"Whether you have an interest in law enfor̶ ̶̶̶̶ ̶̶̶̶
things Nevadan, or just want to enjoy a good book that you w̶̶ ̶̶
want to put down once you start reading it, you'll find *Patrolling the Heart of the West* to be a memorable read. Highly recommended."
    —Excerpt from Readers' Favorite, review by Kimberlee J Benart

"*Patrolling the Heart of the West* is a thoroughly entertaining and enlightening read. With a style reminiscent of the war stories exchanged during a law-enforcement family barbecue, Raabe's skill as a storyteller is evident as he imparts his wisdom and experience with a unique sense of humor, candor, and insightfulness."
    —Andy Brown, author of *Warnings Unheeded: Twin Tragedies at Fairchild Air Force Base*

"Told with great humor and compassion, Raabe's tales show us the heart behind the badge."
    —Michael Gurian, *NY Times* bestselling author of *The Wonder of Boys*

"*Patrolling the Heart of the West* is a quick, entertaining and informative glimpse into an important, sometimes dangerous career spent in a unique, little understood corner of the country."
    —Ed Pearce, Senior Reporter, KOLO-TV Reno

"Raabe tells his experiences with excellent accuracy, grace and wit. I couldn't put the book down!"
    —Colonel Michael Hood, Nevada Highway Patrol

Patrolling
the
Heart
of the
West

Patrolling *the* Heart *of the* West

True Tales of a Nevada State Trooper

Steve Raabe

Latah Books
Spokane, Washington

Book design by Gray Dog Press and Andrew Juarez

Cover image derived from Adobe Stock photos

ISBN: 978-0-9997075-2-4
Library of Congress Control Number: 2018932810

Cataloging-in-Publication Data is available upon request

Manufactured in the United States of America

Production by Gray Dog Press
www.graydogpress.com

Published by
Latah Books, Spokane, Washington
www.latahbooks.com

The author may be contacted at snowraabe@gmail.com

This book is dedicated to my three children,
Timothy Lee, Michael Lawrence, and Corrie Jo,
and to my wife, Janelle Snow,
all of whom spent many years
watching me strap on a gun and leave for work
knowing it was possible I might never be home again.

Contents

Introduction

From family gatherings to sitting around campfires with friends, I have enjoyed sharing the true events I experienced as a state trooper. The stories were well-received, and many friends and family members encouraged me to write them down, so I took their advice.

It is my hope that these stories will help people understand the duties, dangers, and experiences of state troopers patrolling the remote highways of the western United States. Some of my tales are funny, others are sad; some describe people who experienced an unbelievable amount of luck, and others who had no luck at all.

My career covered the last two decades of the twentieth century and into the new millennium. During this period, great strides were made in the field of policing. From protective equipment and speed detection, to computers and portable hand-held radios, improvements were made.

When I started as a trooper at the ripe old age of twenty-three, all citations and reports were hand-written. The escalation of force against a combative subject went from hands-on, to a night stick, to a firearm. In recent years, the police taser has been added as another level of non-lethal protection, but to us it was science fiction.

Nevada State troopers always worked alone. Those of us stationed in rural Nevada were often the only trooper working for over a hundred miles in any direction. During the first decade of my career, we had no portable radios. The car radio was our only option to make contact with anyone. Calling for help outside of the patrol car wasn't possible, and even if it had been there was seldom anyone close enough to respond anyway.

Every winter, snow covered the solar panel that powered our radio repeater located at the top of Maggie Peak. This lone repeater provided radio coverage for the last one hundred miles of State Route 140 to the Oregon State line. When the radio went down while working accidents or arrests, we would give civilians the phone number to dispatch and ask them to drive to the nearest telephone and relay our needs.

I'm not sure exactly how many traffic stops or contacts I made over the course of my career, but when I start estimating the number of citations, mechanical repair orders, verbal warnings, accident scenes, arrests, and motorist assists, it numbers in the tens of thousands.

While techniques, equipment and procedures changed over the years, one thing remained fairly consistent—human nature. Of my countless interactions with people throughout my career, the following stories are the ones that stand out, my memory of them refreshed by my daily diary which I kept religiously. Sometimes my notes were followed by a smiley face, a sad face, brief comments, or simply my favorite word—"Bingo"—when things came together unexpectedly.

Sadly, many of my interactions were with people who were critically injured or recently deceased. I was often asked questions like, "How do you handle that?" or "Don't the death and injuries bother you?"

Any seasoned law enforcement officer has been in too many of these situations to count. Yes, they are sad, but if one is deeply troubled by them, they might be in the wrong business. Besides, death is every bit as natural as birth. Since the beginning of time, humans have been killed in accidents. Whether it was the careless caveman who fell off the cliff, or the knight whose horse dumped him on his head, or the young teen texting while driving, accidents are going to happen. Through enforcement of traffic laws, accidents are reduced and lives are saved, but no one can prevent them all. The hardest situations by far were witnessing the death of those who were beyond help and seeing the grief and sorrow of their family and friends.

I am proud to say that during my career I never had to seriously injure anyone. I engaged in a few wrestling matches and I used compliance holds regularly, but that's about it. I never had to use pepper spray, strike a blow with a night stick, or fire a weapon at any person. That doesn't mean I didn't come close to using these options, because I did. I attribute my record to luck, patience and diplomacy. Luck in that those who wished to hurt or kill me were never given the opportunity, patience by delaying action and using time to my advantage, and diplomacy by talking people into handcuffs rather than forcing them.

Few of the true stories in this book rose to any great level of importance. Most simply reflect another day in the life of a rural, western state trooper going about his daily tasks. You will notice that my personnel (identification) number changed during my career. I was assigned #376 out of the academy, number #144 in the mid-eighties, and #067 when numbers were realigned in the late nineties.

I thank you for your interest in my true tales, and I hope that you will enjoy reading them as much as I have enjoyed writing them.

Sincerely,

Lt. Steven E Raabe (retired)

Nevada Highway Patrol, ID #067

From Garbage Man to Trooper

Being married and a father at eighteen years of age came as a surprise. One of the greatest women I ever knew, my mother Charlotte, wasn't overly excited about my being married at such a young age, but she was absolutely giddy at the prospect of having a grand baby. One of her favorite sayings (of which there were many) was, "The first baby comes anytime, and the rest take nine months."

The fact that I wasn't ready to be a father didn't seem to matter. My priorities changed rapidly from beer, bull riding and fun, to work, diapers and formula. My new son, Tim, seemed to enjoy eating, so getting a better-paying job became a priority.

My new father-in-law, Ray Mack, worked as a truck mechanic at Capital Sanitation. Ray's boss offered me a job, which paid more than I was making, so I became a garbage man. I was given a large aluminum can with a shoulder hook attached to it. My job was to collect the trash from the side yards of two or three homes and carry it back to the truck. The insufferable work was hard, heavy, dirty, and cold, but it paid the bills. Our customers left us beer and bottles of alcohol at Christmas, but I doubt that any would have introduced us to their daughters.

Early one winter morning I met my first Nevada State trooper. I was learning to drive the large garbage truck and inadvertently drove past the pre-determined stopping point. The lead driver, who started each day by smoking weed, insisted that I back the truck up in the dark. After a brief argument about the inability to see, I jumped into the truck and slammed it into reverse and hit the accelerator. I ended

1

up pushing a big, four-door sedan through a fence and onto the front lawn of a house. I was amazed that the car didn't slow the Peterbilt cab-over truck down in the least and that I didn't feel a thing.

The sun was coming up when the state trooper finally arrived, sur-veyed the situation, and started laughing. I failed to see any humor in what had just occurred. The news he delivered hit me like a ton of bricks. The car I had just smashed into was an unmarked patrol car belonging to Carson City Sheriff, Pete Rasner. My real boss showed up and reminded me I was not licensed to drive a truck that large. Know-ing I was on my way to jail, I remember my good fortune when the sheriff stepped out onto his front porch in his robe and said, "It's too early in the day to deal with this. Have your insurance company take care of it."

In the fall of 1976, I moved to Oregon to work for my father-in-law's brother, Gerald Mack. Jerry was a contract timber faller. I ran a chainsaw every day, cutting limbs from downed trees and turning them into logs. After one year I moved to Salem and began work as a drywall finisher. I made good money until the bottom dropped out of construction in the spring of 1980. With a wife and two young sons, I moved back home to northern Nevada. If I was going to be unemployed, I preferred to do so at home.

In the summer of 1980, I was twenty-three years old and making a meager living in Reno delivering furniture. Early one morning, my older sister, Marcie, called and told me that the Nevada Highway Patrol was hiring for trooper positions. I had never thought about becoming a state trooper. At eighteen years of age I had applied and interviewed to become a Reno police cadet, but the fake identification in my wallet took care of that.

I completed an application at the highway patrol office in Reno and a few weeks later I was scheduled to take a written exam and a physical agility test. I was concerned with the written exam, but not the physical test. I was in excellent shape as I had been running eighteen miles a week with my brother, Bruce.

Testing day arrived on a Saturday and I was surprised at the large number of applicants who showed up. The written exam was given first, and only those who passed could take part in the physical exam that followed. I was pleased to have passed the written exam, but a bit discouraged that a couple hundred people were still competing. I passed the difficult physical agility exam which eliminated many more applicants, but there were still plenty left. Then we learned that twice as many applicants had tested in Las Vegas that same day. I decided to take each day as it came, do my best, and see what happened.

Several weeks passed before I received a letter to appear for an interview at the Reno Highway Patrol Office. It was hard not to get my hopes up, even when I considered the number of applicants I was competing against.

On the day of my interview I was shown into a small office. A man in a dress suit entered the room and introduced himself as Peter Zadra. Mr. Zadra was a serious, unsmiling, older man, with short hair and a strong, chiseled face. He appeared quite fit and acted as if no other man on the planet existed. I learned later that Mr. Zadra was actually Colonel Zadra, a battle-hardened Marine Corps veteran and the chief of the Nevada Highway Patrol.

I was nervous, and my anxiety grew considerably when he asked the first question.

"Mr. Raabe, why is it you do not have Nevada license plates on your car? You are required by law to obtain Nevada registration within forty-five days of becoming a resident."

The car actually belonged to my mother who had passed away. I was required to obtain signed documents from my older brother and sister giving up their rights to the car before I could license it, and I actually had all of the required paperwork with me and intended to take care of the problem that day. The highway patrol shared the large building with the driver's licensing and registration offices. I showed Zadra the paperwork and was able to dodge that bullet, but the next shot followed immediately after.

"Mr. Raabe, the Electrolux Company tells us that you did not finish paying off the vacuum cleaner you were buying on credit. Is that true?"

"No sir, it is not true," I said. "I ran out of sheetrock work and sold my truck to pay off all of my bills. Electrolux was paid off and it irritates me that they would say that."

"Are you easily irritated, Mr. Raabe?"

"No sir, I'm not. But I had to sell my truck and start driving the little car that belonged to my mother in order to pay everything off, including Electrolux."

I happened to have the final receipt from Electrolux in my wallet and dodged bullet number two.

"So Mr. Raabe, you are a drywall worker?"

"Yes sir, I am," I replied.

"Then you must have a temper."

"Sir, I'm a drywall taper and finisher. I'm not a hanger."

"Oh, so you're telling me that hangers have tempers and tapers don't?"

"I have been in the drywall trade for four years. Very few jobs have ever gone right. I wouldn't think that a taper with a temper would get much done."

"Well," he said. "I am a licensed general building contractor and I happen to know many sheetrockers. Have you bid any drywall jobs since you moved back to Nevada four months ago?"

"Yes sir, I have."

"You know that it is against the law to bid a job without being a licensed contractor, don't you?"

"Yes sir, I do."

By now I was completely over being nervous. There was no way in hell this man was going to offer me a job, so I figured I would just "shoot the bull" with him until he told me to leave. We ended up talking about construction, Nevada, and a little about the highway patrol. I figured he was just being polite and ending on a good note before he ushered me out the door.

"If you were to get hired," he asked, "what makes you think you could make it through our difficult academy?"

"I have a wife and two boys," I told him. "Failing your academy wouldn't be an option."

A few minutes of conversation passed before Mr. Zadra said, "From our talk this afternoon, I see you are a very honest person. If I were to offer you a job, could you start the academy in six weeks?"

Still figuring this man was pulling my leg, I told him, "Sure, sure I could."

"All right then," Mr. Zadra said. "See the sergeant in the next room and he will give you paperwork that needs to be completed and returned, as well as instructions regarding your training, where and when to show up, and a list of what you are required to bring with you."

To say I was astounded would be an understatement. My new career was about to begin, and I was as excited as a young man could possibly be.

I began the academy on September 15, 1980 in Stead, Nevada, just north of Reno. It was the Nevada Highway Patrol's largest academy class ever and it turned out to be a very difficult, disciplined environment. Our lead instructor had been a Marine Corps drill sergeant at Parris Island, South Carolina, and that's how the academy was run.

I was competing with thirty-three cadets, most of whom were older, many who had prior law enforcement experience, and several who were college graduates. Not having had any college or prior law enforcement experience, I knew I was at a disadvantage, so I worked very hard. I finished the academy in fourth place academically, while in our daily physical training no one ever beat me running in speed or distance.

The academy was over, and this little piggy was going to Winnemucca.

That's Why I'm the Sergeant

Learning to be a state trooper is both exciting and stressful. I knew little about police work when I was hired and was surprised at the amount of training required to perform the job. Hours were spent in the classroom every day, covering topics too numerous to mention. Beyond the classroom were simulated traffic accidents, traffic stops, shootings, first aid, driving courses, range time, self-defense, and physical training. Cadets gain needed knowledge in role-playing exercises, but the real learning takes place on the highway.

Those of us who graduated from the academy now had to look forward to three months of the Field Training Officer (FTO) program. This FTO program is the actual hands-on training of a new rookie trooper who is paired with an experienced training officer. The first week, the rookie rides with the training officer and observes them performing their standard duties. Beginning the second week, the rookie works while the training officer teaches, appraises, and documents their actions. The FTO is there to teach rookies and keep them alive long enough for them to learn what they need to work independently.

Your FTO can make or break you. They are your immediate supervisor, evaluator, and can recommend your dismissal from the job based on performance. I was fortunate to have two outstanding troopers as training officers. Trooper George McIntosh and Trooper Rick Bradley were experienced, respected, and each moved up the ranks throughout their careers.

Less than two weeks into my training, I arrived for my first Friday night shift. It was quite a surprise to find I would work the shift with my new sergeant, Mike Curti. It seems my training officer, Trooper McIntosh, had requested the night off. This unfortunate bit of news raised my stress level tenfold. He seemed nice, but I didn't know yet how to do my job! I wasn't looking forward to this night at all.

It was mid-December in the high desert and the weather was a constant drizzling rain expected to turn to snow later that night. After the first hour completing paperwork in the office, we were ready to hit the road. The sun had set, and it was dark and dreary. It was also the first time I'd ever engaged in police work at night. Please God, I thought, don't let me forget to grab my flashlight.

I can only guess my new sergeant sensed my discomfort. We were going to work US 95 north. Rather than head directly out US 95, we took an alternate route by way of Reinhart Road. Sergeant Curti explained that he preferred this detour so that he could spotlight mule deer hanging out by the Humboldt River. A deer hunter myself, I started to think that maybe the night wouldn't be so bad after all.

The lesson of the night turned out to be issuing what we called "Mickeys"—patrol slang for Mechanical Repair Orders (MROs) issued to drivers of vehicles with obvious problems. Mickeys included inoperable tail lights, headlights, bald tires, and broken windshields, just to name a few. A "Mickey" did not involve a fine or an appearance in court. It required the registered owner to correct the problem, have the repair inspected and signed off by an officer, then mail the Mickey to NHP headquarters in Carson City within ten days. Failure to do so, according to the warning on the back of the document, could cause further enforcement action being taken.

Imagine my surprise as a lieutenant many years later when I learned that nobody kept track of Mickeys being returned or signed off. They went directly into the trash within minutes of hitting the desk at highway patrol headquarters. The lesson taught to a new officer was that a mechanical violation is an easy, valid reason to initiate a traffic stop. This action often resulted in discovering every other violation you can think of. There have been many wanted criminals and DUIs arrested because of a non-working tail light.

We worked Highway US 95 for several hours, then switched to Interstate 80 west. Here I first learned the wit of a man whom I came to admire and respect. At about 2100 hours, we stopped a car traveling eastbound on I-80 twenty miles west of Winnemucca for an inoperative tail light.

With my new sergeant in tow, I approached the vehicle where I obtained the driver's license and registration. We returned to the patrol car where Sergeant Curti promptly resumed his place behind the steering wheel. Not driving yet, I was relegated to the passenger side of the car. I grabbed my Mickey book and stepped outside to fill out the repair order, my trooper hat with plastic cover protecting me from the drizzle.

After several minutes, Sergeant Curti leaned over and asked, "Trooper Raabe, why are you standing in the rain writing a Mickey?"

I leaned into the patrol car and told my new sergeant, "Proper officer safety requires that you not be caught sitting in a patrol car if someone tries to shoot you."

Sergeant Curti, obviously not concerned about dying that night said, "I guess that's why I'm a sergeant and you're a trooper."

I finished writing the Mickey in the dry, front passenger seat of Sergeant Curti's patrol car with the door ajar. Mission accomplished, and lesson learned.

Sawed-Off Shotgun

As a new trooper, I remember arriving code three at the first motor vehicle injury accident I handled on my own. I got out of my car and heard someone say, "Everything's okay now, the Highway Patrol is here." If that person knew how terrified and stressed I was, he would not have been so happy to see me.

Did most of my training show up when I needed it? Yes. Was the fright replaced over time with a bit of swagger? Yes. Could a trooper back down, show weakness or quit when situations got out of control or dangerous? No! Were we occasionally scared shitless when situations went south? Yes!

In the academy, you practice shooting, defensive tactics, weapon retention, takedowns, handcuffing, body searches, riot control, baton maneuvers, approaching vehicles . . . the list goes on. Sadly, many of these techniques were developed because of other officers losing their lives. The infamous Newhall massacre was a tragic incident that led to some of these changes.

In April 1970, four California Highway Patrol officers were killed within minutes of each other outside of Los Angeles. Two officers died first in a shootout with bad guys. Two more officers coming to their aid were shot and killed a few minutes later. The lesson learned was to never rush into an unknown situation without due caution.

On the highway, troopers awkwardly put to use what they learned in the academy. The first job of the FTO is schooling rookies on survival until officer safety becomes routine. This story is an example of an

FTO saving a young, inexperienced trooper's life. The life I'm referring to was mine.

Both Troopers McIntosh and Bradley taught me to patrol ten miles an hour under the posted speed limit. Patrolling under the speed limit is advantageous to the officer. First, patrolling slowly gives the trooper more time to read the license plates of passing vehicles and determine if the license plate is missing or expired, if it's dirty or unreadable, if the plate has been stolen or mounted improperly, etc.

Another good reason to patrol slowly is that it allows the trooper a better look at the occupants. Do they fit the vehicle, are they afraid to pass the patrol car, do they look away as they pass, do they stay behind the patrol car or take a remote exit to get away?

The third good reason to patrol slowly is so that the trooper can thoroughly check out the vehicle. Are there visible mechanical issues? Is the windshield broken, tires bald, windows broken out, door locks or trunk locks missing?

On New Year's Day 1981, I was assigned to work day shift with Trooper Rick Bradley. We were patrolling I-80 west of Winnemucca near the Cosgrave Rest Area. I was traveling at 45 mph, ten under the ridiculously slow, federally imposed speed limit of 55, when I noticed a four-door sedan come up behind us and then suddenly slow down. The vehicle followed us for a few minutes and then proceeded to pass on the left. It was apparent when it passed that the Idaho plates on the vehicle had expired. Two men and a woman occupied the vehicle. They all stared straight ahead and never looked in our direction.

After a brief discussion, Trooper Bradley had me turn on the emergency lights and pull the car over. The vehicle pulled to the right road edge, and I stopped behind it. Both Trooper Bradley and I stepped outside. The driver exited his car and met us near the front of the patrol car. Officers now request violators stay inside their vehicles, but back when I started this technique wasn't standard procedure.

The driver was tall, skinny, blond, and disheveled looking—like life had been hard on him. I told him why I had pulled him over and asked for his driver's license and registration. He pulled his driver's license from his pocket and handed it to me. He told me the vehicle registration was in the glove box and asked if he could go get it. I told him to go ahead.

The young man started towards the passenger side of his car and Trooper Bradley asked me in a hushed and serious voice, "What the hell are you doing?"

"What?" I asked.

"Never let someone walk up and get into their vehicle without you being hot on their ass watching every move. Get up there!"

I hurried and caught up to the young man just as he opened the passenger door. He went for a 20 gauge sawed-off shotgun lying between the seat and the door. It may sound silly, but I had practiced fast-drawing my duty weapon for several weeks at home and I drew my gun faster than he could grab his shotgun.

I yelled, "Gun, stop, I'll shoot!"

Sensing I had the drop on him, he stopped about one second before being dead. Trooper Bradley, with gun drawn, moved up to a position just behind the driver's side rear door. All occupants gave up and we took them into custody.

The sawed-off shotgun barrel was found in the back seat along with the hack saw used to cut it off. It is a felony to have a shotgun with a barrel shorter than eighteen inches in length. We checked wants and warrants on the occupants through NHP Dispatch who advised that the two men had been released from an Idaho prison three days prior. Both were already listed as suspects in the robbery of an Idaho sporting goods store. The two men were found guilty of possession of stolen property and possession of an illegal weapon and became residents of the Nevada State Prison in Carson City. The young woman wasn't charged with a crime.

A Field Training Officer is vital to the trooper trainee and can often be the difference between death and survival. Later in my career, I was an FTO for several years. It was a lot of additional work and responsibility, but I enjoyed it very much. And never again did I let anyone get back into their vehicle without, as Trooper Bradley so expressively put it, "being hot on their ass and watching every move!"

You're Killing Me

I spent my first thirteen years as a trooper in the rural duty station of Winnemucca, Nevada. The part of Nevada I patrolled was large, consisting of over 400 miles of highway and covering 10,000 square miles of remote desert and mountains. Winnemucca, the county seat, had a population of six thousand people. The rest of the district was made up of a handful of smaller communities, an occasional ranch, bar and gold mine.

Yes, I said gold mine. Mines in northern Nevada produce the vast majority of America's gold. The gold mines vary in size, but many are quite large and provide work for hundreds of people.

Living in and working out of a small community as a law enforcement officer is both a blessing and a curse. It's a blessing because you're surrounded daily by friends, neighbors and acquaintances. It's a curse because sometimes you must stop, cite, or arrest friends, neighbors and acquaintances. The key to a successful career in a small town is treating residents fairly. If a traffic violation is minor, a warning is usually enough to change behavior. Often, I would tell locals, "This one's on me. The next one's on you." Officers with a heavy hand did not fare well in small communities.

State Route 140 is a long, remote highway connecting north central Nevada to southern Oregon. Located fifty miles northwest of Winnemucca off State Route 140 was the AMAX Gold Sleeper Mine. Some high-quality gold at AMAX was discovered above the surface of the ground. I used to hunt rattlesnakes in the same area before the discovery of gold there and I've often joked about tripping over gold nuggets while trying to find a rattlesnake.

One afternoon, I was on patrol near the AMAX mine. It was close to the end of my shift, so I started back towards Winnemucca. I had just passed the mine road when a truck pulled onto the highway behind me. Designed with two seats, the crew cab truck was occupied by several miners headed back to town. I was patrolling at the posted speed limit of fifty-five miles per hour.

In 1974, the Federal Government passed the Emergency Highway Energy Conservation Act. This mandate set a maximum speed limit of 55 mph on all highways nationwide. Nevada residents disliked the federally imposed 55-mph speed limit, and state troopers tasked with enforcing the ridiculous law didn't like it either!

At that speed it didn't take long for the pickup to catch me. At the time, the only two vehicles on this open stretch of highway were the mine truck and my patrol car. After following my patrol car for a few miles, the mine truck signaled to pass me. It was a rare day when someone passed a patrol car doing the speed limit.

After pulling even with my front door, the man in the front passenger seat rolled down his window. He sheepishly motioned for me to do the same. The truck had four miners in it. The two miners on the right side both had concerned looks on their faces. I slowed and lowered my window, and the driver leaned forward to shout at me. It was one of my best friends, Starr Harmon.

"Are you going to drive fifty-five miles per hour all the way to town?" he yelled at me. "My God, you're killing me! My son has a Little League game, and I'm the coach. At this speed I'm never going to get there on time!"

Looking serious and trying not to laugh, I yelled back. "Starr, you're in luck. I was just pulling off the road to finish some paperwork. Make sure you don't break any laws on the way to town."

I pulled off the highway and sat smiling as the mine truck continued down the highway.

Two Vanilla Cones, Please

It was July 4th 1981, a boiling hot day with temperatures over 100 degrees. I was patrolling US 95 and stopped a commercial tractor-trailer combination in beautiful, downtown McDermitt for a reason I no longer remember. As luck would have it, the truck stopped in front of the Snack Stop. It was the only ice cream stand for seventy miles in any direction.

Before we had portable radios strapped to our bodies, we turned on a loud speaker when we left our patrol cars. To contact dispatch, we would have to return to the patrol car and use the microphone. But with a speaker on, we could usually hear dispatch call us.

I walked up to the front of the tractor to speak with the driver. With the noisy tractor engine running, there was no way I could hear the outside speaker on my patrol car. While writing the driver a citation, NHP Dispatch called repeatedly to tell me the commercial vehicle had been reported stolen. When I finally returned to my patrol car, a worried dispatcher advised me of the situation. The tractor-trailer serial numbers matched NCIC (the National Crime Information Center) records confirming that both vehicles were stolen.

I placed the driver under arrest for possession of stolen vehicles, cuffed his hands behind his back, and searched him for weapons. After placing him in my patrol car, I contacted dispatch and requested a commercial tow truck respond to take possession of the stolen vehicle. The only tow truck for a commercial vehicle this size was seventy-two miles away in Winnemucca. On a good day, this tow company moved slower than a herd of turtles. We were in for a long, hot afternoon.

After completing the required paperwork, I moved my prisoner from the hot patrol car to one of the Snack Stop picnic tables located in the shade. The longer we waited, the hotter it got. Watching customers eating ice cream added to our misery.

I asked my prisoner to stand up and moved his cuffed hands from behind his back to his front. The two of us walked up to the window where I ordered two large vanilla cones. After placing an ice cream cone into one of his cuffed hands, I walked him back to the table. There the two of us sat. A truck thief and a state trooper, eating ice cream cones together on a hot summer afternoon. When the tow truck finally arrived, I transported my prisoner to Winnemucca and booked him into the Humboldt County Jail.

Coincidentally, the local police department was currently under investigation for abuse of prisoners. These embarrassing stories had recently aired nationwide on the CBS news program "60 Minutes." Not long after, the truck theft case went to court and I was called to testify. Though I was a state trooper and had nothing to do with the local police department, our district attorney felt the need to ask me on the stand if I had bought my prisoner an ice cream cone after I arrested him. I testified in court that I had indeed bought the man an ice cream cone. The judge loved it, and everyone in the courtroom laughed, including the defendant!

It turned out the truck driver had been fired by his boss over the phone and refused to return the truck. He'd been brokering his own loads and hauling them all over the nation for months before he was caught. I don't know what became of him, but he certainly couldn't accuse me of prisoner abuse!

You Bought a Cow

Investigating traffic accidents is a large part of a state trooper's job. Types of accidents troopers handle are often dependent on where they are assigned. Troopers assigned to Reno or Las Vegas will typically work freeway accidents resulting from driving under the influence, unsafe lane changes, disregard of traffic control devices, and speed. Accidents common to rural Nevada are driving under the influence, falling asleep, being distracted while driving, and striking animals in the roadway. Animals most often hit are cattle and deer.

Most rural two-lane Nevada highways are posted open range, meaning that cattle have the right to be on the highway and drivers must watch for them. All rural troopers handle several vehicles vs. animal accidents each year. One reason to investigate traffic accidents is to identify the cause and find solutions to reduce the occurrence. To reduce the number of range cows hit, one trooper suggested they be equipped with battery powered tail lights.

Late one evening, NHP Elko Dispatch sent me to a car versus cow accident on US 95, three miles south of McDermitt. This part of US 95 runs through the Fort McDermitt Paiute and Shoshone Indian Reservation, and cattle on this section of highway were common. When I arrived, I observed a large deceased cow off the east roadway edge. A passenger vehicle with extensive front-end damage and a broken windshield sat in the northbound travel lane.

The driver, an older man from California, was uninjured but quite upset. He said he didn't see the cow until it was too late and demanded to know who owned it. I informed the driver that he was now the owner of the cow.

He gave me a puzzled look and said, "No, I want to know who owns this cow, because I will sue their pants off for letting it run loose on the highway."

Once again, I informed the driver that he owned the cow. "This is open range," I explained. "As soon as you hit that cow, you bought it!"

I then gave the driver more bad news. What was once a normal, straggly, old range cow had now turned into an expensive Paiute show animal. Drivers were always surprised to learn that they were the new, proud owners of what, until recently, was referred to as livestock!

Did You Kill Anyone?

I was dressed, in my patrol car, and backing out of the driveway in a matter of minutes. Dispatch advised, "Notification time 0213 hours."

Dispatch had called me out to check on a pickup truck stopped on I-80 just west of Golconda, and as described, a Dodge pickup was parked right in the middle of the westbound travel lane. It had a high lift kit, big tires, and its lights were still on.

I crossed the median, turned on the emergency lights, and stopped behind the truck. The engine was running, and I saw a person in the driver's seat. I walked to the driver's door and peered inside the pickup with my flashlight. A man was sleeping with his head against the window. And another detail caught my eye. On the seat next to the man's right hand was a holstered gun.

I tapped on the window with my flashlight and yelled at the man, "Nevada Highway Patrol! Wake up!"

The man, drunk and unimpressed, opened his red bloodshot eyes, looked at me for a brief second, and then resumed his nap.

I stood there for a while contemplating my next move. Secure the gun so the guy couldn't grab it? Turn off the engine so he couldn't drive away? Remove the drunken guy from the truck as soon as possible? Which to do first?

I didn't want to reach up and over the sleeping drunk to grab the gun. Nor did I want to reach over the man to turn off the ignition key. Opening the door and pulling the drunk out onto the ground seemed a practical option. This action would keep him away from the gun and the gas pedal. So that's what I did!

The man was young, with dark hair and a beard. He looked strong enough that if he decided to wake up in my arms and fight, I could be in for a ride. Knowing I would need both hands for this brilliant plan, I slipped my flashlight into the ring on my belt and then pulled the door handle. The man, leaning heavily against the door, fell into my arms. I handcuffed him in a hurry and placed him into a seated position on the ground. The man barely noticed being removed from his truck and didn't seem to care. I secured him in the back seat of my patrol car.

After shutting off the man's truck engine, I moved the holstered gun and gun belt to the front passenger floor of my patrol car. The tow truck arrived and took possession of the pickup truck. Next, it was off to the hospital for a legal blood alcohol test.

The Humboldt General Hospital at four in the morning is a quiet place. My prisoner, drunk but awake, was friendly and cooperative. A Winnemucca police officer arrived a few minutes later with his own drunken driving prisoner. We both completed legal blood draw requests and the lab tech drew the blood on both subjects.

The city officer and I walked our prisoners out to our patrol cars and discussed having coffee after tucking them in for the night. I decided to put my cooperative prisoner in the front passenger seat for the short ride to jail and opened the door to move the holstered gun to the back seat.

Though this event occurred over three decades ago, I remember it as if it happened last night. I picked up the gun belt and the leather sling that goes over the hammer came loose. The gun slipped out of the holster and headed for the ground butt first. Except the butt of the gun wasn't happy to just hit the ground! Oh no! It had to fire off one round when it hit! Holy cow!

I turned to see if my prisoner was shot. I looked right past him to the city officer and his .357 magnum pointed my way.

"Don't shoot!" I yelled. "Misfire!"

After checking my prisoner and myself for holes, unloading the firearm, and apologizing to everyone present, the dumbass state trooper and his prisoner headed off to the jail.

Now the 4:30 a.m. phone call to my sergeant. I was not looking forward to this conversation. The phone rang and Sergeant Curti answered. It sounded as if I had awakened him.

"Sergeant Curti, this is Trooper Raabe. I need to inform you that I fired one round over the roof of Humboldt County General Hospital."

"How in the hell did you do that?" said my suddenly wide-awake sergeant. I explained how this mishap occurred and waited for a response. In an annoyed and sarcastic tone, Sergeant Curti asked, "Did you kill anyone?"

"Not that I know of," I replied.

Sergeant Curti ended the conversation by saying, "Trooper Raabe, be in my office at ten o'clock this morning."

I radioed off duty as the sun came up, intending to go to sleep but finding it impossible. Less than four hours later I would have to report to Sergeant Curti's office to receive my first butt kicking. I had never been in trouble at my job before. This would be a new experience.

In uniform and back on duty, I arrived at the office at ten o'clock sharp. I sat in front of Sergeant Curti, ready to take my lumps.

Sergeant Curti looked at me and said, "I have one question for you, Trooper Raabe. Why didn't you unload the gun the first time you touched it?"

I thought about the question and replied, "That is a good question. I wish I had a good answer."

Sergeant Curti didn't seem angry, nor would I say he was disappointed. I think he saw the situation as a rookie trooper who made a mistake, which could have turned out a lot more serious than it did. With a stern look on his face he said, "Trooper Raabe, I want you to think about how you might have handled this situation better and safer than you did. Now go home and get some sleep!"

I never made that mistake again, and I went on to serve more than ten years in supervisory positions, both as a sergeant and lieutenant. That short meeting with Sergeant Curti and his one simple question taught me more about being a good supervisor than any other experience of my career. Don't punish an honest mistake when the action can be corrected in a positive way.

I worked for several poor supervisors. The worst were micromanagers insecure in their positions. Many punished and made examples out of employees when it wasn't necessary. Either they didn't have a Sergeant Curti to show good leadership or they were too impressed with themselves to listen. I'm guessing it was the latter.

On Our Way to Court

Every trooper in Nevada had their own patrol car assigned to them. My first patrol car was a 1978 four-door Plymouth Fury. The Fury came with a 440 cubic inch engine, automatic transmission, and an extra-large alternator to run the radios and lights. Big and fast, my Fury was a remnant of the past. It was one of the only highway patrol cars at the time to still have a screen separating the front and back seats.

When it became mine, it had plenty of miles on the odometer and was on the verge of being worn out. No snot-nosed trooper deserved a new patrol car until they'd spent some time working the road. The three-year-old Fury wasn't the nicest patrol car, but it was mine.

Every day, highway patrol troopers drive fast. You can't catch someone speeding on remote highways unless your speed is considerably greater than theirs. The first time I drove the Fury above 100 mph, my hands gripped the wheel with white knuckles and a rapidly beating heart. I kept thinking it would be terrible to crash at that speed.

Thankfully, the feeling of impending doom didn't last. Before long I was cruising between 100 and 135 mph several times a day with one arm out the window, singing to the AM radio, and jotting down notes as I went. Driving became automatic for me.

I called the Fury "the sailboat." Once it got above 100 mph, it rocked back and forth as if riding waves on the ocean. Thankfully, I-80 had two lanes in each direction. The sailboat often used both lanes as it swayed side to side. Steering and stability were not its strong points.

The Fury had an amazing amount of room, with a super-sized trunk capable of carrying an unbelievable amount of gear. The passenger compartment was big enough to transport a driver (me) and four adults. One weekday morning, I had the chance to fill it up with a whole row of drunks.

On patrol on I-80, I noticed an older, four-door Lincoln Continental headed west while using both travel lanes. The Lincoln, going under the posted speed limit of 55 mph, got my attention. I knew it wasn't having a high-speed steering problem similar to the sailboat. I followed the Lincoln to the top of Golconda Summit and saw that there were four older adult men in the car, two men in the front and two in the back. I activated the emergency overhead lights, and the driver took his sweet time pulling over.

As I approached their car, I noticed them passing around a bottle of booze. When the driver rolled down his window, I smelled the odor of alcohol and the sound of men laughing and joking with each other. I asked the driver how much alcohol he had consumed, and he replied, "All of us have had way too damn much!"

As the stop progressed, I learned several interesting facts. The group had started their journey at a bar in Battle Mountain and now the driver and all three of his passengers were drunk. One of the passengers was a defendant in a DUI trial scheduled to begin at 10:00 a.m. in Winnemucca Justice Court. In fact, all four of them were on their way to court, one as a defendant and the other three in drunken support of their friend. Only four really drunk guys could come up with such an enormously stupid idea!

I happened to be the only trooper on duty for miles in any direction so there was no one coming to assist. The driver was placed under arrest for driving under the influence. One at a time, I removed the other three from the vehicle and placed them under civil protective custody, meaning they were too drunk to turn loose. They would spend at least eight hours in jail until they sobered up enough to take care of themselves and would then be released. I handcuffed all four and strapped them into the sailboat for the trip to town.

To these four men, all on their way to jail, I was merely an inconvenience. The booze disappeared into my trunk, but the party never stopped. These guys told jokes, made fun of their current dilemma, and laughed until they cried. Hell, I laughed until I cried. I never had so much fun arresting a group of men in my entire career.

By the time we got to the jail my cheeks were sore from smiling and laughing. The party continued at the jail until all were booked and tucked away into their separate cells. I called the court and told them that their defendant for the 10:00 a.m. trial wouldn't be showing up. Never again did I have a patrol car large enough to transport four men to jail at one time. And never again did I have the opportunity to transport such a fun bunch of drunks to jail.

A Dead Cop's Grave

I had been out of the academy for less than a month and was learning my new job as a state trooper under the direction of Trooper McIntosh. McIntosh was very good at his profession, and I was lucky to have him as my training officer. Like me, he was a Nevada boy, and while he was the tough, serious, no-nonsense type, we got along just fine.

In the early morning hours of January 6th, 1981, Trooper McIntosh and I were called out to an injury accident east of Winnemucca. The ambulance arrived at the scene of the rollover minutes after we did and transported all the vehicle's occupants to the hospital before we could talk to them. As soon as we finished the on-scene investigation, we proceeded to the Humboldt County Hospital to meet with the driver and get a statement. As we walked into the hospital, a nurse stopped in the hallway and stared at us as if she had just seen a ghost. It was an awkward few moments, and after an uncomfortable amount of time, she turned and walked away.

After completing our business, we returned to our patrol car in the hospital parking lot. McIntosh asked if I remembered what he'd told me about the Nielson family earlier in the week and I nodded, recalling his warning to be extremely careful during any dealings with the Nielsons or the criminals who hung out with them at their bar. None of them were fond of cops.

"The nurse who gave us that long look is Liz Nielson," Trooper McIntosh explained. "She and her husband, George, own the Paradise Bar."

Located twenty-two miles north of Winnemucca on US 95, the Paradise Bar was a rundown building made of rock and mortar. Many of its patrons were drunks, cowboys, fake cowboys, poachers, thieves and misfits.

George Nielson, a California transplant, had recently run across our sergeant, Mike Curti, at a local restaurant and told him, "If any of your troopers stop me or my friends, we're more likely to pull out a gun than a driver's license."

The year before, Trooper McIntosh had occasion to enter the Paradise Bar on business and he received a very cold reception. While in the bar, McIntosh noticed several bobcat hides hanging from a pole. A trapper himself, McIntosh knew they were new hides and poached out of season. McIntosh alerted Nevada game wardens who came down hard on the Nielsons. This certainly didn't help the relations between the local state troopers and the Paradise Bar patrons.

Later that morning, I was called out from home again and told to meet Sergeant Curti at the Winnemucca office. When I arrived, most of my fellow troopers were already there. The day before, a friend of the Nielsons named Claude Dallas had murdered two Idaho Fish and Game officers at a remote camp north of Winnemucca.

Dallas had set up camp in Bull Basin, on the South Fork of the Owyhee River. This part of the Great Basin Desert is very remote, with little around except a few ranches. Most of the ranchers have permits, issued by the Federal Government, to graze their cattle in different areas.

About ten days before the murders, the son of a local rancher who grazed cattle in that area stopped by Dallas' camp. While speaking with Dallas, he spotted illegal bobcat hides and a poached deer. When warned by the son that Idaho Fish and Game would be checking the area, Dallas said, "I'll be ready for them." These ranchers had problems with poachers before, so when they had a chance, they notified Officer

Bill Pogue, described what the son had seen, and warned him to be careful.

Pogue, and fellow Idaho Game Warden, Conley Elms, approached Dallas' remote camp. They confirmed that game violations had occurred and told Dallas he was under arrest. When Elms went into Dallas' tent to secure the illegal bobcat hides, Dallas shot Pogue with his .357 caliber handgun. When Elms came out of the tent, Dallas shot him as well. After both men were down, Dallas grabbed a .22 caliber rifle and shot one bullet, execution style, into each of the game warden's heads.

Jim Stevens, a friend of Dallas, was at the Bull Basin camp when the murders took place. He witnessed the entire event, and helped Dallas transport the bodies up to the truck. Conley Elms was a big man, and his body fell off the pack horse on the trip out of the canyon, so they left him. Dallas and Stevens loaded up Pogue's body and headed for Paradise Bar.

That same day, late in the afternoon, Dallas and Stevens showed up at the Nielson's with the body of Officer William Pogue in the back of the truck. Dallas was close with the Nielsons, using the Paradise Bar address as his own. The Nielsons even furnished Dallas with food and supplies while he trapped and poached deer in the deserts of southern Idaho and northern Nevada.

The Nielsons saw Pogue's body and loaned Dallas their truck, shovels, and a pick so that he could bury the officer in the desert. Dallas left the Paradise Bar with the body, buried it, and then returned the truck. The Nielsons let Dallas have a one-day head start to disappear before they revealed the crime to law enforcement. It was no wonder Liz Nielson stared at us when we walked into the hospital. She was keeping one hell of a secret and must have thought we were there to see her.

For several days, McIntosh and I searched for any sign of Claude Dallas. We assisted sheriff's deputies as they searched through cabins, mines and ranches. Claude had disappeared, but the FBI was on his trail. I have always said I would rather have two trained street cops than four FBI agents if I needed help taking down a carload of bad guys. But if someone is on the run, there is no one better in this world at finding them than the FBI. Still, Claude managed to stay on the loose for fifteen months. We heard several times throughout that period that the FBI almost had him, but he had managed to get away before they captured him.

Fifteen months later, in April of 1982, I was responding to a reported drunk driver on US 95. As I passed the Paradise Bar, I noticed a helicopter flying low over a trailer house, a mile north of the highway. It appeared to be a military type aircraft and it definitely got my attention.

I continued on my call, arrested an Idaho man for driving under the influence, and took him to the Humboldt County Jail. When I walked him into the jail, I saw several men standing around in military fatigues. They had just caught Claude Dallas at his friend's house, not a mile from the Paradise Bar. Dallas, who supporters claimed would never give up, attempted to escape in a pickup truck. A bullet, fired by a friend of mine, passed through the bottom of the driver's door striking Dallas in the foot. The pickup stopped, and Dallas crawled out into the sage brush and surrendered.

Claude Dallas was transported back to Idaho and held in jail until his trial which began in mid-September 1982. Three weeks into the trial, Dallas testified that he had buried William Pogue's body off Sand Pass Road north of Winnemucca. He said he had crossed the cattle guard, followed the fence line to the north, and buried Officer Pogue near the end of the fence. As soon as Dallas testified to this fact, the media ran out of the courthouse, on their way to the confessed burial site.

It was decided that law enforcement officers would guard the reported crime scene area and keep the media one-quarter of a mile away on Sand Pass Road. Two officer teams, working four-hour shifts, parked near where Dallas said he had buried Officer Pogue, keeping everyone away. I and another state trooper had the last watch from four until eight in the morning. There were media vehicles parked all over Sand Pass Road as this was one of the biggest criminal cases of the early eighties. Reporters who strolled too close to the area were threatened with arrest.

By the end of my shift, the crime scene team led by Detectives Chuck Rikalo and Bob Milby of the Nevada Division of Investigation arrived to begin their work. They were both veteran detectives, and I was pleased when they asked if I could assist them in processing the crime scene.

After a briefing describing how the team was going to work the scene, we began. A large, rectangular area, about half the size of a football field, was plotted with posts located at each corner. Everyone involved took a handful of long wooden stakes with red plastic ribbon tied to the top of each. Walking side by side, at five-foot intervals, we planted a flag everywhere we found anything that looked like it didn't belong in the desert.

It wasn't long before we started to find small pieces of cloth, all of them the same color. With the amount of cloth we were finding, something, or someone, was definitely close by. We continued the grid search until a couple of minutes later someone yelled, "Here he is!"

There was no doubt about it this time. The remains of a human body were found. Pogue's body had been buried face up in a shallow grave. The skeletal remains of his right thigh and pelvis areas were uncovered and exposed to the elements. The coyotes had gotten to the exposed parts and scattered them around, but luckily most of the body was still there. The head, upper body, left abdomen, left leg and both feet were still buried in the sand. We taped off the area, took photos, diagramed the site, and located the exact location of the body by triangulation measurements to the fence.

We laid out tarps and started to dig. Every shovel full of dirt exposed more of the game warden's skeleton and was screened through a crime scene sifter box which separates dirt from evidence. As we sifted, we found uniform buttons and other evidence suggesting that the body was that of a law enforcement officer. There was no doubt this was the body of William Pogue, but until it was scientifically confirmed, through prints or dental records, you are only allowed to assume. The entire body had decomposed underground, leaving only skeletal remains except for his feet which were still intact inside the heavy work boots he'd been wearing. It was a strange site to see a skeleton wearing boots.

It was my turn to manually shake the sifter. Shaking each shovel full of dirt was suspenseful as we were at the point where each shovel full revealed something. I got to the last of the sand in one scoop and found a .22 caliber bullet. The execution bullet Dallas shot into Pogue's head.

Dallas had made many friends in this part of Nevada and people believed him to be some great mountain man who could live off the land. Originally from Ohio, Dallas had grown up reading Louie L'Amour novels and moved out west to live his dream. When he showed up in our part of the world, he didn't know the front of a horse from the back, but he learned. Dallas also had an aversion to any law, or any lawman, that kept him from shooting or trapping any animal he wanted to, at any time. The boy from Ohio was now living in the big, remote Great Basin Desert and he didn't think he had to follow any rules.

Dallas testified that Pogue was aggressive, kept his hand on his gun, and that he had feared for his life. The Idaho jury bought the story and found him guilty of voluntary manslaughter and using a firearm in the commission of a crime. The judge wasn't quite so naïve and sentenced Dallas to the maximum of thirty years.

Dallas escaped from an Idaho prison in March of 1986. He was on the run for a year, and all of his supporters were convinced he was living off the land, somewhere high in the mountains where no one would ever find him. In March 1987, the FBI captured him in Riverside, California. He was caught coming out of a 7-11 store with a sack of groceries in hand.

Claude Dallas served twenty-two years and was released from prison in 2005. He was given an eight-year reduction in his sentence for good behavior.

When Claude Dallas was caught the second time in Riverside, California, I wrote a poem to the editor of the Humboldt Sun newspaper in Winnemucca. It was 1986 and I was tired of hearing people talking about Claude Dallas like he was some expert survivalist. He was a trapper, like hundreds of other trappers who lived in our area. He was nothing special, just a guy who camped in the desert, shot deer out of season, and killed two law enforcement officers.

Ode to Claude's Friends

It makes them feel important,
Part of history today.
I knew Claude; he's a real nice guy,
Set him free, I've heard them say.
When Claude escaped from prison,
His friends all thought they knew,
He was living off the land eating game,
Doing what mountain men do.
And oh, did it break their ignorant hearts,
Some to the point they cried.
When their mountain man was caught with two sacks of food,
At a market in Riverside.
Turn him loose, he's a real nice guy,
I've heard some folks around here say.
Let's hope no one they know, is shot in the head,
By a real nice guy someday.

Now I Know My ABCs

I can't tell you how many times I've heard the story of an officer asking a DUI suspect to recite the alphabet backwards. I am convinced the story is an urban legend.

The idea behind any field sobriety test is to show the court that the subject could not complete a task ordinarily simple for a sober person. There is nothing simple about reciting the alphabet backwards. An officer might be asked to show any test that was given to a defendant before the court. This is another reason to keep tests simple.

Field sobriety testing usually included asking the suspect to recite the alphabet from A to Z. The ABCs are generally followed by having the suspect balance on one leg while counting to twenty-five and then walking heel to toe in a straight line while counting to ten. Throughout the entire test, the officer records the suspect's ability to follow directions.

One would think that reciting the ABCs is a simple thing to do. After all, most children can recite or sing them in their proper order before beginning first grade. But for a person impaired by too much alcohol, it can be far from easy. The more intoxicated the person is, the harder simple tasks become.

I've arrested hundreds of drunk drivers in my career as a trooper. The recitation of the ABCs has always been the funniest part of the field sobriety test. I have heard so many renditions, I could never remember them all. But the better ones I will never forget.

Among my favorites was a large, young logger from Alaska who finished his recital by singing, "Now I know my ABCs, next time won't you sing with me." I remember smiling and thinking that he'd better hope there's not a next time.

Another man only got as far as K before pausing and then saying, "And all those other mother f@#kers." The night did not end well for him.

Yet another young man left out several letters between A and Z. When I brought this fact to his attention, he asked, "Did you want the long version or the short version?" I told him I wasn't aware there was a short version, and if he wanted to try again I preferred the entire alphabet. His second try was another short version, so the night did not end well for him either.

State troopers take the offense of driving under the influence seriously. We must deal with the death and destruction these people cause. But that doesn't mean we can't laugh a little at the expense of the drunk who is on his way to jail.

Rural American Justice

Early one summer morning, I was working traffic on US 95 near Orovada, Nevada. This little spot in the desert is just south of the Oregon-Nevada state line, hence the name. I clocked a green, two-door Dodge with Idaho license plates traveling northbound at a high rate of speed. I stopped the car north of Orovada and made contact with the driver.

While writing the young man a traffic citation for 90 mph in a 55 zone, wants and warrants were checked through my dispatch center. The dispatcher advised that this young man had outstanding warrants in Idaho for failure to appear in court for traffic violations.

When given this information, an officer's options become very limited. The warrants were issued for misdemeanors from another state, so I could not arrest him in Nevada for those. Having proved he would not honor his promise to appear in court, I could not turn him loose. I was left with only two options: arrest him for speeding and transport him 60 miles to the jail in Winnemucca, or try to find Oren MacDonald, the Justice of the Peace in McDermitt, Nevada. McDermitt was much closer and meant no booking or arrest reports later.

Near 7:00 a.m. I requested dispatch call Judge MacDonald's house on this beautiful, early Saturday morning to see if he was interested in seeing us. Dispatch soon advised that the judge was awake, coffee was brewed, and that he was awaiting our arrival. The young man followed me twenty miles to Judge MacDonald's house.

We parked our cars in his driveway and together we approached the front door. Judge MacDonald answered the front door wearing his black judge's robe over the top of his pajamas. He invited us in and proceeded to the kitchen table where his gavel was sitting. He asked me if I wanted some coffee and I said that I did. The young man asked for coffee and Judge MacDonald advised him that he was a defendant and not allowed coffee in court!

Judge MacDonald set a hot cup of coffee before me and took a seat. He picked up his gavel and slammed it on his kitchen table, stating, "Court is now in session."

I was expecting a simple posting of bail on the citation with a court date to follow, but before I figured out what was truly going on I was being sworn in as a witness. Judge MacDonald asked me to describe the events of the morning, which I did briefly and to the point. He read the charge of speeding, 90 in a 55-mph zone, and asked the young man how he pled. The young man said he'd never been in court before, so he didn't know what to plead. This was quite apparent from his numerous failures to appear.

It's really very simple," Judge MacDonald explained. "If you're guilty of speeding, you plead guilty. If you're innocent of speeding, you plead not guilty. How do you plead?"

"Well, I was speeding," the young man replied. "So, I guess I plead guilty."

Judge MacDonald asked the young man how much cash he had, and the young man counted his money which added up to $120 and some change. Judge MacDonald said, "Your fine for speeding in Humboldt County, Nevada is one hundred twenty dollars."

The young man handed the money across the kitchen table to Judge MacDonald who slammed the gavel and said, "Court is no longer in session."

Since court was officially over, Judge MacDonald got up from the table and poured the young man a cup of coffee. Knowing the young man was going home to Boise, Judge MacDonald asked him how much gas he had in his car. He said he planned on topping off his tank in McDermitt. Judge MacDonald slid twenty dollars across the table and told him to fill up. The judge asked him if he'd eaten breakfast and he replied that he had not. The judge slid another twenty dollars across the table and told him to get something to eat.

After the young man was given a receipt for the payment of his eighty-dollar fine, the three of us visited and finished our coffee. This was a dying, now extinct, example of rural justice delivered American style. God, I miss those simpler days!

Just a Hitchhiker

I arrived at the vehicle rollover on I-80 at 2318 hours, forty-two minutes before the end of my shift at midnight. It had been a typical May evening. I had made a few traffic stops, but no accidents to investigate, until now. The accident occurred just west of Winnemucca, on the eastbound side of the highway. It was reported that the vehicle had been abandoned, and no one was at the scene.

The only vehicle involved was a blue Chevrolet pickup with a camper shell atop the bed and completely filled with stuff. The marks on the highway indicated a typical off road, overcorrected, rollover accident. The Chevy had damage to both sides and the top. After rolling, it had come off the roadway and landed on its wheels in the dirt.

It was dark, and no one was around. No driver, no witness, not a soul. Just me and a wrecked truck with California license plates. I asked Elko Dispatch to contact the Winnemucca hospital and find out if anyone might have come in for treatment. The answer was no. I began thinking this was probably the result of another drunk driver who'd wrecked their pickup and walked away so that they wouldn't be arrested.

I had been there about five minutes when I heard moaning coming from the camper shell. The items inside started moving and the moaning got louder. I heard someone say, "Help me, help me get out!"

I lifted up the back door to the camper and saw a man's face sticking out of the jumble of mess in the back. "What happened?" he asked.

41

"I was about to ask you the same question," I said.

"I don't know," he replied. "I was hitchhiking in Reno and this guy picked me up and let me ride in the back of the camper."

"Where is this guy?" I asked.

"I don't know anything about him. I was riding in the back and I guess we were in an accident. I hit my head and just woke up and called for help. Maybe he caught a ride or walked into town to notify the police."

"I didn't see anybody walking into town as I drove out," I said.

"I just woke up and I don't know how long we've been here," he added.

"Do you need to go to the hospital?" I asked.

"Yes, I think I should be checked out."

"Do you have identification on you?"

"No," he said. "I don't have any identification."

I asked him his name, date of birth, and his social security number and wrote down the information he gave me. He identified himself as Jeffrey Richards, of Los Angeles, California.

"Is there anything in this truck that belongs to you?" I asked.

"Just a backpack in the back," he replied.

I opened the back of the camper and there was a backpack within reach.

"That's it," he said.

I grabbed the backpack and looked through it for weapons and identification. It contained nothing but clothes and toiletry items.

Rather than call out the volunteer ambulance, I asked a Winnemucca police officer to pick Mr. Richards up and transport him to the hospital, two miles away.

After shipping Mr. Richards off to the hospital with the police, I called dispatch for vehicle registration information and to request a tow truck. Dispatch advised that the vehicle, a blue 1982 Chevrolet pickup, was registered to Donald Knight, with an address in Yuba City, California.

I completed my work at the scene, and as soon as the tow truck arrived, I left for the hospital. Mr. Richards had been checked out in the emergency room and released. Other than a few bumps and scrapes, he was just fine.

There was still no contact from any driver. I couldn't hold Mr. Richards for anything as it's not against the law to not have identification, so I asked him where he wanted to go. He said he would just get a room for the night and move on tomorrow.

I offered to drive him to a motel, and he said that would be great. As I approached the main part of town, he asked me to just drop him off at a casino and he would get a room later. I pulled up to the front entrance of the Winner's Inn Casino, opened the door to my patrol car, said goodbye, and let him out.

I made a right turn, drove about one hundred feet, made a U-turn, and pulled into a large, dark parking lot. I turned off the lights and sat for while with a great view of both the Winner's Inn front and side doors.

Not five minutes later, I saw Mr. Richards walk out of the casino. As luck would have it, he walked to the same corner I had just turned right at, went down two blocks and into the office of one of several motels located on that street. I watched as he spoke with the motel clerk, filled out paperwork, and was handed a key. He left the office, walked down to room #28 on the first floor, and closed the door behind him.

I pulled my patrol car in front of the motel office and walked inside.

"Hello," I said to the clerk. "There was a man who just registered for a room a few minutes ago. How did he pay for the room?"

"He paid cash," the clerk said.

"Could I see the registration form he filled out?" I asked.

The clerk handed me the form. The clerk had just rented the room for one night to a Mr. Donald Knight from Yuba City, California, signed, sealed and delivered. Bingo!

I knew the man had no weapons, so I figured I could do this one alone. I knocked on the door, and Mr. Knight asked who it was.

"It's the motel clerk," I said. "I need you to sign one more paper."

I heard the door unlock, it opened slightly, and I helped open it the rest of the way. I had him in handcuffs in record time.

Surprised, he asked, "What's this all about?"

"Well Mr. Knight, you are under arrest for obstructing and delaying a peace officer in the performance of his duties, fraud for being treated at our hospital under a false name, failure to maintain a travel lane, and anything else I can come up with."

"I just paid for this room," he said.

"I have a nice room for you at the jail," I told him.

When I ran a driver's license check in California under his real name, it was suspended. He also had several misdemeanor warrants which couldn't be served in Nevada, but it still made for a fun night.

Contact the Railroad ... Never Mind

One summer morning, Elko Dispatch called my home at 2:15 a.m. and advised of a traffic accident in the small township of Golconda. A citizen reported a pickup truck upside down on the highway near the Union Pacific Railroad crossing.

I arrived thirty minutes later and located the accident vehicle. It was an older, tan, Chevy pickup truck resting on its roof. It wasn't near the crossing as reported; it was directly on top of the railroad tracks.

I parked my patrol car twenty-five feet from the pickup and looked for the driver, but found no one. The truck contained several beer cans and smelled of alcohol. This was looking like the usual drunk rolls car, leaves the scene, and reports the car stolen in the morning scenario.

I returned to my patrol car and told dispatch to inform the Union Pacific Railroad of the circumstances. Seconds after hanging up the microphone, a train whistle sounded. I looked up and saw a westbound freight train, with horns blaring and brakes screeching as it slid toward the pickup. This was going to be amazing to watch, I thought, and I was not disappointed. The train struck the pickup truck right in front of my patrol car, and knocked it so far down the tracks, I lost sight of it. As the train was using the usual half mile to grind to a stop, I advised Elko Dispatch to forget contacting the railroad about the truck as they'd already found it.

After the train stopped, I walked along the tracks and stood in front of the engine. I immediately made three observations. First, the engine had sustained minimal damage to the steel handrail that went around the front walkway. Second, an engine is enormous when standing on the tracks right in front of it. And third, "I am not kidding when I say" an engine is enormous when standing on the tracks right in front of it. The pickup truck was in pieces on the south side of the tracks. It had gone from moderate rollover damage to being demolished by a train!

I met with the conductor and engineer who provided statements. After finishing photos, a field sketch, and turning the pickup over to the tow company, I stopped by the registered owner's home in Golconda. No one was home, so I proceeded to the next possible place to locate Mr. Jackson—the only bar open at 4:00 a.m. for thirty miles in any direction, Waterhole #1 in Golconda.

With help I located the elusive, intoxicated Mr. Jackson sitting on a stool. Mr. Jackson said he was drunk when he'd rolled his pickup. Because he no longer had a pickup to drive, he had to walk to the bar. Several witnesses confirmed that Mr. Jackson arrived at the bar intoxicated and told everyone he had rolled his truck. I arrested Mr. Jackson and gave him a ride to the Humboldt County Jail. After getting him a room and tucking him in for the night, I headed for home

The next day, I told my friend Dennis Mastin, a conductor for the Union Pacific Railroad, about the train hitting the truck. Dennis asked if I carried battery jumper cables in my patrol car and proceeded to teach me how to use jumper cables or any conductive metal to stop a train. Low voltage electricity travels through each separate rail. Connecting a wire or piece of steel to each track sends the engineer a red light signaling the train to stop in that section.

Troopers should be instructed in this simple procedure to stop a train. Had I known, I could have warned the engineer and saved a Chevy. Then again, I got to see a pickup fly and that was worth not knowing!

Bopped on the Noggin

As an academy cadet, I trained on a baton called a straight stick. After a couple of years working the road, the straight stick was replaced by the PR-24. Though the PR stood for "Prosecutor," we referred to it as the Public Relations 24. A hard, plastic baton, the PR-24 was twenty-four inches long with an attached side handle six inches from one end. It was both an effective defensive and offensive weapon.

I never struck anyone with a baton during my career, but I came close on several occasions. One of the close calls occurred one morning in Winnemucca. I hadn't left town yet when I noticed a passenger car on Winnemucca Blvd being driven in an erratic manner. The car sped up, slowed down, and used both travel lanes as it went. I turned on the red and blue overhead lights and the driver pulled the car into a motel parking lot and stopped.

I contacted the driver, a well-built white male who smelled of alcohol. The physical signs of intoxication were all there—slurred speech, flushed complexion, poor balance, and a confused mind. Giving the driver a series of field sobriety tests was next on the list. Normally, near the end of the series of tests, if I intended to arrest the driver, I would ask them to do one last test. Lean backwards with both arms extended behind their back, close their eyes, and count to ten. I would handcuff the person before they made it to ten. This technique limited their ability to fight or resist arrest.

I had a wary drunk this morning. It was clear I wasn't going to sneak the cuffs on him, so I simply told him he was under arrest for driving under the influence of alcohol. The man thought this was a terrible idea and told me so. He said that if I tried to arrest him, there was going to be a fight. I told him that being turned loose was not an option. If he chose to fight, he'd be charged with resisting arrest and go to jail by way of the hospital. Reasoning with an intoxicated person is rarely successful, but I tried anyway. The brief conversation went nowhere. I told the man to turn around and place his hands behind his back.

The man puffed up his chest, balled up his fists, and said, "The fight is about to begin."

I removed my PR-24 from its ring, spun it around perfectly, and tucked it into the underarm position. I'm glad the spin looked as good on the road as it did in PR-24 class. "If you don't do what I ask, I'm going to have to hurt you before you go!" I said.

I waited for him to come at me as he took a few seconds to consider his options. At last he turned around and placed his hands behind his back. Whew, a close one! I handcuffed him in a hurry before he changed his mind.

During the booking process at the Humboldt County Jail, I kept thinking how lucky I was that I didn't have to fight this guy. He seemed determined to fight and then all of a sudden just gave up. I looked at his booking photo taken the last time he had been arrested. The man had a big, red lump right in the middle of his forehead. Records indicated he chose to fight with police during his previous arrest. Somewhere in his intoxicated mind he had just enough memory of the big lump on his forehead to realize that he didn't want another.

Baa Baa Black Sheep

One summer morning, the Nevada Highway Patrol Dispatch Center called me at home and advised of a commercial vehicle fire on I-80 westbound near Golconda. The rig was reported as a cab-over tractor, semi-trailer, and a pull trailer. Both trailers were loaded with several layers of live sheep.

When the driver noticed that his overheated brakes had caused a fire in the rear trailer, he'd pulled to the side of the highway, ran back, and detached the burning trailer from the semi-trailer. After moving the tractor and semi-trailer farther down the highway, the truck driver ran back to the burning trailer and opened the doors in an effort to save the sheep,

I arrived at this chaotic scene in the early pre-dawn hours. The pull trailer was still on fire and partially loaded with sheep. The sheep that had escaped the inferno, some of them partially burned, were running in and out of traffic. As the Golconda Fire Department fought the fire, I spent numerous .357 rounds shooting injured sheep. The morning turned into one big, ugly, sad mess!

When the fire was under control and the situation calmed, my next task was to find a place to hold scores of loose sheep. I asked the truck driver to follow me to the fairgrounds in Winnemucca to unload the semi-trailer full of sheep. We would place the sheep into corrals and return with the empty trailer.

It took an hour and a half to travel to Winnemucca, unload the sheep, and return. Upon returning to the scene, a Golconda fireman ran up to me and told me that a big, fat ewe had been stolen. Allegedly, two men grabbed the ewe, tied its legs, and put it into the back of a red Chevy El Camino. The sun had been up for an hour and the fireman pointed to a red Chevy traveling eastbound on I-80. The El Camino was three miles east of our present location climbing up Golconda Summit, and off I went in pursuit of the sheep bandits.

Seven miles east of the accident scene, I stopped the El Camino. As I walked to the driver's door, I saw a nice, fat ewe lying in the back of the truck. I wish I could have heard the conversation going on inside the truck. Both men looked as if they had been caught with their hands in a cookie jar.

I asked the driver where they'd gotten the ewe, and he replied that they'd found it on the side of the highway. Didn't you see the dozens of other sheep with it, I asked. Both men shook their heads no. Sheep are a herd animal. When they're scared, they travel in a flock. Sheep on the outside of the crowd try to get to the center. The ones in the center of the crowd do their best to stay there. I asked the men if they planned on delivering this sheep to the lost and found at the Sheriff's Office. They didn't answer the question.

These two idiots were taking valuable time out of my already busy day. I explained to them that I didn't know how much a sheep cost. Under Nevada law, if the ewe was worth more than a hundred dollars, they had committed a felony. If worth less than a hundred dollars, they had committed a misdemeanor. I explained to them that if I were in their present dilemma, I would turn around and put the sheep right back where I'd gotten it!

I followed the two sheep thieves back to the scene of the crime. They pulled to the side of the road, removed the ewe from the back of the truck, untied it, and gently pushed it toward the desert. After the ewe found its friends, the two men headed for their car. I asked the men where they were going, and they said they were late for work. I told the men that they were already at work.

Not understanding my comment, one of them replied, "We really are late for work. We should have been there by now!"

I explained to them that had they not stopped to steal a sheep they wouldn't have been late, and I gave them two options. One, herd and catch sheep this morning, or two, go to jail for stealing sheep this morning. Either choice worked for me.

Both men elected to chase, herd, and capture sheep. Not happy at all, they grumbled and complained until the job was done. What started as a sad situation ended with a laugh watching these two dummies running across the desert chasing a flock of sheep! I'm sure that those two men will never forget their short careers as sheepherders. Nor will I. Baaaah!

I See What You Mean

Driving on snow and ice is dangerous. Practice and experience increases one's chances of having a successful trip in inclement weather. But even with years of experience, it doesn't take much to throw a driver off their game and have that safe trip turn into a bad night.

Even with winter driving knowledge and experience, my patrol car and I would occasionally find ourselves in places where we had no intention of going. With luck, these mishaps occurred without damages or a witness. Each year, when the first storm arrived, I would find an empty parking lot to practice my winter driving. Getting your winter wheels under you in an empty parking lot is a good way to start the snowy season. Besides, it's fun!

When big storms hit in rural Nevada, troopers spent little time at home. Our days consisted of car wrecks, novice drivers, stranded motorists, tire chains wrapped around axles, stopping traffic, and waiting for snowplows. These storms insured extra-long shifts, call outs from home, and plenty of overtime!

These are my rules for driving on ice:
1. Don't accelerate too fast.
2. Don't brake too hard.
3. Don't oversteer.
4. Don't shift into another gear with gusto.
5. Turn the front wheels in the direction of the skid.
6. And the most important rule of all, Slooow Dooown!

A big problem on icy highways is four-wheel-drive vehicles. Are they better in bad conditions? Yes. Are they less likely to break traction and slide? Yes. Can they travel faster than vehicles without four-wheel drive? Yes, for a while at least. But eventually the laws of fate will catch up to a driver's reckless ways. Two wheels, four wheels, or eighteen wheels do not change the fact that ice is ice!

One snowy morning, on I-80 east of Winnemucca, I was working accident number twelve of the day. Property damage investigations were generally quick and easy. Fill out a form, get statements, determine cause, usually issue a citation, and then head off to the next one.

Two young teenage males had taken seats in my patrol car and were completing accident statements. The passenger involved in the accident, a stocky dark-haired kid, was in the back seat. The driver, a thin blonde kid, was in the right front seat. His father's four-wheel-drive Chevy Suburban was upside down in a concrete culvert off the north roadway edge.

When I asked what happened, the new driver said, "I don't know. Everything was fine and then we were sliding sideways. We ran off the highway into the ditch and overturned."

"How fast were you going when you lost control?" I continued.

"Only sixty miles per hour," he said.

"Sixty miles per hour is way too fast on ice, even with a four-wheel drive," I replied as a Ford Ranger pickup zipped past us on the highway. "Like that truck there. It's going way too fast!"

I reached up, unlocked my radar, and released a radio wave. At the speed of light (186,000 miles per second) the wave traveled the distance to the Ranger (200 feet) and returned. The instantaneous reading registered at 56 miles per hour.

It was readily apparent that the driver of the Ford Ranger had a radar detector. The machine detects the radio wave being sent from the radar and instantly alerts the driver. When hearing the alert, many drivers tap the brakes in a futile effort to slow down.

Let's return to rule number two for driving on ice: Don't brake too hard. As soon as the Ford Ranger's brake lights came on, the vehicle spun out of control and slid from the highway into the median. The vehicle's two right side wheels furrowed into the soft dirt and it overturned onto its passenger side.

When the accident was complete, the young man turned to me with an astonished look and said, "Gosh, I see what you mean!"

We watched as the Ranger's driver door opened toward the sky and a man climbed out. He walked the short distance to my patrol car, took a seat, and waited his turn. His accident report was lucky number thirteen for the day!

Leave Herman Alone

One afternoon, while visiting Region III Headquarters, NHP dispatch requested that I proceed to the hospital to obtain a legal blood alcohol sample. An intoxicated driver who had rolled his vehicle on State Route 225 north of Elko would be awaiting me.

Upon entering the hospital emergency room, I immediately heard the voice of a very disagreeable man. He was strapped down to a gurney and screaming at three nurses who were doing their best to calm him down and assess his injuries. Since he was already upset, I felt it best that he not see me, so I stayed out of his view. I walked into the back of the room where they were treating him, explained to one of the nurses why I was there, and began filling out the paperwork required to obtain a legal blood alcohol sample.

Three nurses were busy running around getting vital signs and checking the drunk out. One of the nurses told the man that she needed him to urinate so they could look for blood in his urine. Blood in the urine can be an indicator of more serious internal injuries. The nurse kept asking the man to pee for her. The more the nurse asked, the more obnoxious and belligerent the man became.

"I need you to pee," the nurse continued.

"I told you, I don't have to pee," the drunk said, followed by a string of profanities.

"We're trying to ensure that you aren't injured, so I really need you to pee."

"I'm not peeing for you or anybody else," the drunk shouted, followed by more profanities. There was a pause and then I heard him say, "Hey, what are you doing? What are you doing to Herman? Hey, you leave Herman alone!"

I looked over as the nurse took hold of the man's privates and began painting the guy up with some sort of colored antiseptic.

"You leave Herman alone! You leave Herman alone!" the drunk kept shouting.

The three nurses grinned as they all looked at each other in disbelief. They tried not to laugh out loud as they silently mouthed the words, "Herman? Herman?"

Meanwhile, the lead nurse stood over the drunk while working some kind of tube.

"Ow! Ow! I told you I don't have to pee! Ow!!!"

"Don't worry about it, sweetheart," the nurse replied. "You're peeing right now whether you have to or not."

It was about this time I made a promise to myself. If I ever have to go to the emergency room to be treated, I promise I will be on my best behavior. I will not upset the nurses and I will not have any type of name for any of my body parts!

Put Your Seatbelts On

Most people don't know there are a series of actions taken by law enforcement officers when investigating a traffic accident. We refer to them as, "The thirteen steps of accident investigation." Most everyone has driven past an accident and looked on as a trooper rolled a measuring wheel down the road. If you have seen this, you've watched step number eight in progress, "Diagram the scene." This story has to do with investigation step number three, "Handle emergencies."

One afternoon, at 1435 hours, dispatch notified me of a serious injury accident on I-80 at the Imlay Interchange thirty miles west of Winnemucca. With lights blaring and siren screaming, I made my way to the accident scene. Upon arrival, I noticed several cars and a tractor trailer parked on the eastbound side of the highway. It was common for motorists to stop and help at accident scenes. I advised Elko Dispatch that I was on scene and they gave me my arrival time, 1445 hours.

As I exited my patrol car, a person met me and said, "It's a bad one. A woman, a boy and a girl are seriously injured."

Most of rural America's interstate highways are designed the same. The highway includes the entire area within the right of way, which is bordered by fences. It comprises two paved roadways going in opposite directions, an unpaved center portion between them called the median, and the unpaved portions from the outside edge of each roadway to the right of way fence.

Accidents are documented on an official report. To demonstrate how accidents are officially described, I copied the description that follows from the actual report. Vehicle #1 was a red 1985 Renault.

"Vehicle #1, eastbound, I-80, partially left the north roadway edge into the median. Driver #1 steered to the right. Vehicle #1 reentered the left travel lane. Driver #1 overcorrected to the left. Vehicle #1 partially left the north roadway edge. Driver #1 overcorrected to the right. Vehicle #1 crossed the eastbound lanes broadside. Driver #1 overcorrected to the left. Vehicle #1 left the south roadway edge, striking a marker post. Vehicle #1 rolled several times, ejecting all occupants. Vehicle #1 came to rest off the south roadway edge, on its wheels, facing in a southwest direction."

The mother, who was forty-one years of age, came to rest in the dirt, eighteen feet from the east roadway edge. The car rolled over the woman as she was ejected and came to rest fifteen feet beyond the woman. The nine-year-old daughter came to rest ten feet beyond the car, face down in sage brush, suspended three feet off the ground. The seven-year-old son came to rest fifteen feet beyond the girl, face-up in the dirt, on the far side of the right-of-way fence.

Accident step number three, "Handle emergencies," follows steps one and two, "Arrive at scene safely" and "Set up preliminary traffic control" to protect the scene. Step three was, by far, the most difficult and stressful. Rural troopers often found themselves in the middle of nowhere caring for injured people while waiting (sometimes it seemed forever) for an ambulance to arrive. Every Nevada trooper was trained and certified as an EMT. The training was great, but the state-supplied first aid kits were a joke.

A California Highway Patrol officer on vacation stopped to help on a wreck one summer and laughed at our first aid kits. He asked, "Are you kidding me? This is all the medical supplies you're furnished with?" With the generosity of the local hospital and ambulance crew, most of us collected much-needed items our employer failed to furnish.

So here I was with three unconscious, critically-injured patients, and plenty of advice from the good Samaritans who stopped to help. I grabbed my stethoscope and blood pressure cuff and started with the woman. Her blood pressure measured low, and her respirations were weak and shallow. I placed one of the Samaritans beside the woman with directions to monitor breathing and to call me if she stopped breathing or vomited.

Next, I went to check the little girl and take her vital signs. As I approached, I saw a man attempt to move her. I yelled at him not to touch or move her. The man, who I later learned was the driver of the tractor trailer, said he wanted to remove her from the sagebrush. I told him that we needed to leave her right where she was. Not feeling the need to explain my decision to not move the girl, nor having the time to do so, I checked the girl's vital signs. They were not good, but better than her mother's. I instructed the truck driver and others helping to monitor her as well.

I crossed the fence and checked the little boy. His vital signs were the best of the three. Again, I stationed a volunteer to watch him and call me if needed.

As I passed the little girl on the way back to check her mother, the truck driver said, "We need to get this girl out of the bushes."

Again, I told him, "We're not moving her. Please do what I have asked!" The man was not happy, but he did as I requested.

I took the mother's blood pressure and vital signs again. Her blood pressure and respirations had worsened in a very short period of time. This woman was not long for the world. I looked up and saw the ambulance arriving on scene.

When the EMT driver stepped out, I yelled at him to grab the MAST (medical anti-shock trousers). These life-saving pants cover the patient's lower extremities and abdomen. When inflated, blood from the lower part of the body is squeezed and forced upward to the heart and brain where it's needed. My son is an Air Force fighter pilot and wears a similar item called a G suit. Forcing blood into the upper body and brain keeps him from passing out while pulling G's in his jet.

As soon as the pants were fitted and inflated, the mother's blood pressure improved. This bought precious time to get her to the hospital alive. The three patients were stabilized on backboards and readied for transport as quickly as possible.

When the ambulance left, and the excitement was over, the good Samaritans began to leave. Two people claimed to have witnessed the vehicle after it was out of control, but no one saw what caused the accident. One person said he had seen the Renault as it sped past his vehicle a few minutes before.

After completing accident steps 4 through 11 at the scene, I proceeded to the Humboldt General Hospital in Winnemucca. Upon arrival, I learned that the three patients had been transferred by air ambulance to Washoe Medical Center in Reno. I returned to the Highway Patrol Office in Winnemucca to contact dispatch. Certain information had to be relayed to dispatch before going off duty.

The next day I turned on my radio and advised dispatch I was 10-41 (on duty). Dispatch informed me that my accident from the previous day had turned into a double fatality. Both the mother and the little girl had died in Reno. The little boy was stable and conscious. I asked dispatch to send a Reno trooper to the hospital to interview the boy.

The roadway marks from the accident were different from those generally left when drivers fall asleep. I'd seen both many times. The mother had deliberately steered her car off the roadway.

The Reno trooper called me later that day. He told me he met with the six-year-old boy and his father. The boy said his mom had swerved to miss a van. He said that when the car started sliding out of control, his mother had yelled, "Put your seatbelts on!" These were the last words this boy would hear his mother say.

You don't have time to buckle up or jump out of a car after the trouble begins. If you had that much time, you wouldn't be in trouble to begin with. Seatbelts keep you in the car until the crashing and rolling stops. If you have a death wish, don't wear your seatbelt and get thrown out of your car. If you are lying in the ditch after being ejected and you're thinking you are lucky and safe, be sure to make room for your best friend. Who is your best friend? It's your car, and it's traveling the same direction you are. Maybe it wants to share the ditch with you or perhaps it simply wants to roll over the top of you and keep on going.

I wish the story had finally ended there, but soon after, I learned that the truck driver who I'd counseled at the accident scene had somehow contacted the father and told him that I'd done nothing to help his little girl before the ambulance arrived. He told the grieving man that I'd simply left her lying face down in the sagebrush. The father filed a complaint with my department regarding my apparent lack of action. I had to respond to this distraught husband and father in writing describing the scene and my actions.

When a person is severely injured, you move them only if it is immediately necessary to save their life. The little girl was breathing, face down, and in the perfect position to prevent asphyxiation from pulmonary-aspiration not uncommon for people with severe head injuries. A little girl choking to death on her own vomit is not my idea of proper care. Until the ambulance arrived, and I had the equipment and other EMTs to help move her properly and safely, she wasn't going anywhere. Period!

I will sum this story up with one word of advice. Handling all aspects of traffic collisions is what troopers do and they are damn good at it. If you want to help at an accident scene, which is greatly appreciated, do what the trooper asks you to do. Otherwise, you are not helping and are turning into an unwelcome pain in the ass!

She Pulled Herself Over

The vast, rural, Nevada desert creates several inconveniences for a patrol officer. In many parts of our state (the nation's seventh largest in size) there are great distances between towns. On I-80 across northern Nevada, the towns are fifty to seventy miles apart. On secondary state routes, those distances are even greater.

From the city of Winnemucca to the Oregon state line is one hundred and forty-three miles of lonely, desolate highway. Doughnut shops are nonexistent. Fuel stations, restaurants, and every other convenience you can think of are many miles away. These tribulations are factored into your typical day and don't present a problem. But when nature suddenly calls, the problems can begin.

No one wants to think about a neatly dressed, professional state trooper squatting or standing by a bush on the side of a highway. However, it's a common occurrence in the middle of the desert. A motorist witnessing such an event doesn't add anything positive to the state trooper image, so the action must be fast and discreet. With no trees and long straight stretches of secondary highways, approaching traffic can be seen for miles. On I-80, interchanges and underpasses are miles apart, but handy if needed.

I had just answered nature's call at a remote underpass on I-80. It was another beautiful Nevada morning with the sun shining and desert birds chirping. After getting situated back into my office, a 1989 Ford Mustang 5.0, I proceeded westbound on the circular on-ramp and was just taking it easy. As I entered the travel lane, I noticed a passenger vehicle coming up behind me in the fast lane. I had no idea how fast it was going, nor did I care. As the vehicle passed me, I saw the driver was a young woman. The car slowed down, pulled in front of me, and its right turn signal came on. I turned my emergency overhead lights on and we both pulled to a stop on the side of the highway.

I approached the car and watched as the young woman reached into the glove box and removed some papers. This was looking like a self-induced traffic stop. When I reached the driver's door, the young woman handed me her driver's license and vehicle registration. Could this get any easier, I thought.

"Do you realize how fast you were going?" I asked her.

"Yes. Eighty-five miles per hour," she said.

"And you are also not wearing a seatbelt required by law?"

She admitted that she hadn't been wearing her seatbelt, but I decided to only issue her a citation for speeding. She drove away, and as I walked back to my patrol car I thought of a few tips to future violators.

Violator tip number one: Sometimes officers are not paying attention to what you are doing.

Violator tip number two: Never pull yourself over. If the officer wants you to stop, you will know when it happens.

Violator tip number three: If an officer pulls you over and asks how fast you were going, politely say I wasn't paying attention or I don't know. There is always a chance the officer doesn't know either.

The Secretary's Son

For the first several years working out of the Winnemucca office of the Nevada Highway Patrol there were only five troopers. Michael Curti was our traffic sergeant, but all of us, including Sergeant Curti, worked for General Ginger Gabiola, our office secretary.

Ginger, an absolute sweetheart, reminded us daily of scheduled assignments, including court cases, meetings and training. She typed arrest and fatal accident reports, answered phone calls, and ran the office day to day. Having the ability to contact troopers by radio, Ginger acted as the lifeline to our families. If spouses or children needed us, everyone knew to call Ginger.

One particular favor Ginger did for me, though unintentionally, was to quit the Nevada Highway Patrol to raise cattle. Two years later I married her replacement, Janelle Snow, my wife of thirty years.

One spring afternoon, Elko NHP Dispatch contacted me by radio and advised of a serious injury accident. A driver was trapped on US 95, seven miles north of Winnemucca. Twelve minutes later I arrived at the accident scene. As I stopped, a young man ran toward my patrol car. I recognized him as a friend of Ginger's son, Phillip. I had seen them together before at our office. He told me that Phillip was trapped under the car.

The vehicle had flipped upside down and its roof rested on the head and upper body of the partly ejected occupant. His broken leg extended into the passenger area with his foot stuck in the steering wheel.

I had worked hundreds of traffic accidents and didn't think Phillip would live through this one. Already rehearsing how to tell Ginger that her son had died in a traffic accident, I went to the overturned vehicle and yelled, "Phillip, can you hear me?"

I was not expecting a reply and was surprised to hear a muffled voice say, "Yes! Get this sucker off me!"

By now, several motorists had stopped. I removed Phillip's foot from the steering wheel and laid his leg on the ground. Together, the motorists lifted the vehicle while I and another man placed large rocks under it for support. Phillip, in extreme pain, was relieved and grateful to see daylight. When the ambulance arrived, we extricated Phillip and he was transported to the hospital in Winnemucca. After being stabilized in Winnemucca, they transferred him to a larger hospital in Reno.

The vehicle chose a soft, sandy place to land, and Phillip, who should have been squished, would recover. I didn't have to give my dear friend Ginger the horrible news every mother fears. The day ended well.

Who Are You Screaming At?

The middle of June 1985, our local Nevada Highway Patrol Office in Winnemucca hired a brand-new secretary. In government lingo, the position was called an Administrative Aid II. Her name was Janelle Snow Cunningham.

Janelle's new position called for her to split her time 50/50 between the Nevada Highway Patrol Division and the Motor Carrier Division. The Motor Carrier Division licensed and collected fuel taxes on all commercial vehicles operating in Nevada. The one division Janelle did not work for was Motor Vehicle Licensing and Registration, though in Winnemucca we all shared the same building. A person coming to the Highway Patrol had to walk into the Driver's License Office and through another door to get to our office.

The first week or two at a new job is always exciting and nerve-wracking at the same time. Here was this new, pretty, young lady working for the Nevada Highway Patrol. Surrounded by all those mean troopers she had always done her best to avoid. Yes, we had a job that demanded we take charge. And yes, while at work we seem pretty sure of ourselves. But underneath, troopers are pretty much the same as everyone else.

Let me set the scene for you. It's Monday, the first day of Janelle's second week at her new job. It's mid-morning and she is sitting at her desk in the Highway Patrol Office. The adjoining Driver's License Office is empty. The two DMV employees, assigned to the Winnemucca office, packed their stuff and moved their operation to smaller Nevada towns every Monday and Tuesday. The Driver's License Office in Winnemucca was only open for business on Wednesday, Thursday and Friday. I, Trooper Raabe, was working on a lengthy fatal accident report in the back squad room, located two doors down from Janelle's desk.

I hear the door open and close, followed by some conversation. Very soon, one side of that conversation rises in volume. Seconds after that, one side of the conversation had gone from loud to screaming. I could hear our young, sweet, new secretary Janelle saying, "I am sorry! I am sorry! The Driver's License office is closed today! They will not be open in Winnemucca until Wednesday!"

I don't really remember the back of my chair hitting the wall as I scooted back from my desk, but Janelle said that was the first thing she heard. As I stepped into the main office, I observed a very tall, well-built, older cowboy, hat and all, with both hands firmly placed on Janelle's desk. He was hovering above this barely five-foot-tall young lady and screaming about poor service.

As soon as the cowboy saw me, his demeanor changed dramatically. I asked him in a serious, somewhat elevated tone, "Why are you screaming at our new secretary?"

"I need a new driver's license," the cowboy replied. "This is the DMV and there is no one here to help me."

I pointed to the big sign on the window that read, Nevada Highway Patrol, and said, "This is the Highway Patrol Office. Like this young lady has told you, we don't give out driver's licenses here. You'll have to wait until Wednesday, or you can drive to the town of Lovelock if you need something today. Since we're talking about your driver's license, let me have a look at it."

The cowboy handed me his driver's license. I told him to have a seat and that I would be with him in a minute.

I returned to the squad room and picked up the NHP hotline. This was a phone that instantly connected me to any Nevada Highway

Patrol Dispatch Center and NHP office in the state. I called my dispatch center in Elko, Nevada and gave the dispatcher the cowboy's personal information. I asked her to run a driver's license check and run wants and warrants on my cowboy.

No more than a minute went by before I heard the dispatcher say, "Trooper Raabe, your subject is 11-10 Mary with daytime service!" In Nevada Highway Patrol lingo that meant, "Your cowboy has a misdemeanor warrant for his arrest, issued by a Nevada Court that can only be served during daylight hours!" This is when a law enforcement officer feels like standing up and yelling, "BINGO!"

I walked back into the main office and had the pleasure of telling the cowboy, "You have a warrant for your arrest!" Within minutes, and directly in front of our new secretary's desk, I handcuffed and searched our belligerent cowboy. Then out the door we went on our short walk across the street to the Humboldt County Jail.

Our new secretary, Janelle, was very impressed with the young highway patrolman who came to her aid. So impressed, that she spent the next year setting me up with some of her single girlfriends. Two years later, when none of those matchmaking escapades worked out, she finally married me herself. ·

That was thirty years ago, and though she is not quite as impressed with me as she used to be, she is still my girl!

Your Sergeant's My Best Friend

My first duty station on the Nevada Highway Patrol was the small town of Winnemucca which at the time had a population of about six thousand people. Many locals you dealt with in the course of a day were related to, friends with, or worked for someone you knew. In a small town, dropping names was a common attempt to dissuade a trooper from issuing a citation. You know my cousin, so and so. You surely know my friend who works for the Sheriff's Office. Do you know my neighbor? He works for the court.

One afternoon, I observed a bright, shiny, red sports car traveling eastbound on I-80, just east of Winnemucca. The vehicle was traveling at a high rate of speed and I clocked the car on radar at 85 mph in a 55-mph zone. It was apparent the driver saw me because I watched the speed of the vehicle decrease rapidly on radar. I crossed the median, caught up to the vehicle, and pulled it over.

I approached the driver's door, identified myself, told the driver why he was stopped, and obtained his driver's license, registration and insurance certificate. The white, older man was nicely dressed and very polite. He asked me if he could step out of his vehicle. It was not an uncommon practice at the time to let a driver exit their vehicle, so I told him he could, and he joined me at the edge of the road.

I informed the driver that I would be issuing a citation for speeding. As I started to fill out the citation, he told me that he owned several pizza franchise restaurants in northern Nevada, including one in Winnemucca. Then the man said, "Your sergeant, Mike McCurti, is one of my best friends."

I looked at him for a few seconds before I replied, "I don't think I know him!"

"How could you not know him?" the driver asked. "He's the local Highway Patrol sergeant."

I thought for a minute and again said, "I don't believe I've met him. Mike McCurti? Huh, the name doesn't ring a bell."

In a desperate voice, the man asked, "Where do you live?"

"I'm stationed in Winnemucca."

"You're stationed in Winnemucca, with the Nevada Highway Patrol, and you don't know Sergeant McCurti. How can that be?"

"I'm sorry," I said. "I not only don't know him, but I've never heard of him!"

The man was having a difficult time understanding how on earth I could not know the only highway patrol sergeant in this part of Nevada. At the same time, I was having a difficult time understanding how this man could be my sergeant's best friend and not even know his last name. My sergeant's name was Mike Curti, not Mike McCurti!

It was way past time to issue this McDummy a McTicket. If you ever feel the need to drop a name, make sure you get it right!

Mushroom Man

Halloween Day, 1983, a four-year-old girl and a three-year-old boy were traveling on I-80 with their father. In any "normal" family, the kids would be excited about trick or treat and getting their costumes ready. Not these kids, however. They had spent their morning hours drinking wine with their father as he drove them across Nevada on their way back east.

The father, driving a bright red Datsun 280Z, stopped at a convenience store in Winnemucca for fuel and snacks. While in the store, with his two children in tow, the clerk smelled alcohol on the father and thought he was under the influence of drugs or alcohol, or both. The clerk thought the children were acting strange as well and was concerned for their well-being. My involvement began when the clerk called the local Winnemucca Police and reported the situation.

My dispatch center relayed the information to me as an ATL (attempt to locate). The Datsun, bearing Nevada plates, was last seen pulling out of the store parking lot toward an eastbound I-80 on-ramp. I was working twenty miles east of Winnemucca when I received the call, so I parked on the eastbound side of the Golconda Summit Rest Area, turned up the tunes on the radio, and watched traffic go by.

A few minutes later, I spotted the Datsun and yelled, "Bingo!" I fell in behind the car and observed it from a distance. The driver would have been very lucky to see me as he drove past, and he continued on as if he hadn't. The Datsun drifted from side to side in the travel lane, once crossing over the fog line. Good enough for me. I notified dispatch that I had located the ATL Datsun, and that I would be on a traffic stop, eastbound, at the Iron Point Interchange.

I approached the Datsun and met with the driver, a white man, thirty-four years old, with light brown hair and blue eyes. I told the driver that I had seen his car swaying and mentioned the store clerk's concern for his children when he stopped in Winnemucca. I asked if he'd been drinking, and as he handed me his driver's license, he said, "Yes, I've been drinking a little wine. But I'm not drunk."

"What about the children?" I asked. "They appear as if they've been drinking alcohol as well."

"Oh, yeah," he said. "I share a little wine with them from time to time."

"Did you share a little wine with them this morning?" I asked.

"Yeah, a little. It's good for their blood."

I walked around the Datsun to converse with the children. The little girl was in the front seat, and the little boy was sitting in the right rear, surrounded by boxes and clothes with a plastic laundry basket on top of the pile. I immediately noticed the basket was filled with clear, plastic, sealed bags of mushrooms. These were not your normal garden variety mushrooms you find in Safeway. These bags contained hallucinogenic Psilocybin (Magic) mushrooms, a schedule IV controlled substance.

The man's driver's license identified him as Daniel P. Surroz of Stateline, Nevada. Stateline is located in Douglas County, at the south end of Lake Tahoe, and shares a border with California.

I asked Mr. Surroz to step from his vehicle and saw that he was about five feet five inches tall and built like a fireplug. Either he had spent time in prison, or he was a body builder who devoted a lot of time to the sport. Had Mr. Surroz been belligerent, or in the mood to fight, I probably would have had to shoot him. Tasers had not been invented yet.

After submitting to a field sobriety test, I placed Mr. Surroz under arrest for child endangerment, driving under the influence, and possession of a controlled substance with the intent to distribute. Mr. Surroz was booked into the Humboldt County Jail, the mushrooms were marked and detained as evidence, and the children were turned over to child protective services.

Later that day, I met with my counterpart, Rick Cornish, from the Nevada Division of Investigation. Rick informed me that he had spent the day in Lovelock, Nevada, located seventy miles west of Winnemucca. Earlier that day, someone had found a cargo trunk lying in the middle of Main Street and had turned it in to the police department. They believed the trunk had fallen from someone's car as they passed through town. Located inside the trunk were personal items, books on growing mushrooms, and a cigar box containing several New Mexico driver's licenses. Each license had different names, dates of birth, and social security numbers, and all had the same identical photo of one man.

The next morning, I drove to Lovelock and met with the chief of police. The driver's licenses all displayed a photo of my suspect. Bingo again! I returned to my office in Winnemucca, and ran each fake ID for wants and warrants. It turned out that Mr. Daniel P. Surroz, AKA John Daniel Green, Michael Green, Michael Clark, Scott Beaulieu, Ron Hambright, James Raymond Daugherty and Ronald Sanchez, was wanted by numerous local, state, and federal law enforcement agencies across the country under many of these different aliases. Several agencies placed felony holds on my arrestee while he was in jail.

One detective contacted me from Texas and said Mr. Surroz was wanted in his jurisdiction for fraud, under the name of Raymond Daugherty. It seemed that the real Raymond Daugherty's home was burglarized, and his college diploma and other items of value were missing. The crimes against Mr. Daugherty didn't end there. Insurance papers were also stolen, and Raymond Daugherty, the imposter, spent three days in the hospital after undergoing an operation on his hemorrhoids. The real Raymond Daugherty's insurance company contacted him and asked why he didn't get pre-approval for his operation and his prolonged stay in the hospital. Of course, the real Mr. Daugherty asked, "What operation?"

You would think that would have been the end of the story, but it got even better. Three days after I arrested Mr. Surroz (not his real name), the owner of the Stateline apartment he was renting noticed that it was vacant, and the television was missing. He called the police to investigate and when they went into the apartment they found over fifteen-hundred quart jars filled with Psilocybin mushrooms worth over $250,000—the largest find of illegal mushrooms in Nevada history.

I never knew why Mr. Surroz packed up his family and abandoned a quarter of a million dollars worth of drugs. Since the police stumbled onto the drugs, I would guess he had made enemies of the wrong people, and it was leave fast or die.

The amount of illegal, Schedule IV drugs Mr. Surroz possessed was an automatic life sentence in the Nevada State Prison, if convicted. The only way to reduce the life sentence, according to statute, was to become an informer and work for law enforcement. Mr. Surroz went to work for the Federal DEA (Drug Enforcement Administration) and helped round up numerous bad guys around the country. The DEA agents were very happy with the results he produced.

All of this began with a store clerk who took the time to call police when she noticed something wrong with a father and his children. Stay aware and don't be afraid to call the police when something seems strange. In police talk, we call it a JDLR (just doesn't look right).

Young Pups

Seasoned troopers joke about the enthusiasm rookies have for the job when, after six months in the academy, they finally hit the road. There is nothing worse than an inexperienced, new trooper with a full ticket book and an abundance of zest for the job! We dinosaurs remember those days. It took time and experience to learn that law enforcement was a job, not a crusade. Unfortunately, there are a few that never learn, and they usually have short careers.

It was five minutes past midnight (0005 hours), on a warm summer night in Winnemucca. I was training a new trooper by the name of Paul Hinen. Paul was twenty-three years old, and excited to put his new police skills to work. We were just leaving the patrol office when we heard the Sheriff's Office dispatch one of their deputies to an accident at the end of the pavement, on East Second Street. East Second Street is also known as State Route 289. The funny thing about the end of the pavement on SR 289 is that it could fall under either department's jurisdiction. If the accident began on the pavement, it was ours. If it started in the dirt, it was the county's.

Paul perked up like a new pup when he heard the radio call, and asked if we should respond. I assured Trooper Hinen that if the accident was ours, we would know soon enough. It was late, I was tired, and it was past time to go home. If we went off duty before we were called, the day shift patrol unit who was responsible for everything after midnight could respond.

Paul was new and had not had a patrol car assigned to him yet, so he was riding with me. As we cleared the office and turned onto Main

Street, Paul said, "Hey, did you see that tractor-trailer run that red light?"

It was hard not to see as we were the only two vehicles on the road, but I said, "Trucks don't run red lights this time of night. Especially when troopers are on their way home."

"I think we should at least stop and warn him," Paul said.

"Oh God, do you really think so?" I asked. "You can't let this one go so I can go to bed?"

A training officer should certainly not discourage a young eager rookie, but there's always one more stop if you look hard enough.

"Alright, Trooper Hinen. It is against my better judgment, but here go the lights."

I turned on the overhead lights and the tractor-trailer pulled into the parking lot of a business and stopped. My "pain in the butt" and I approached the driver's door as the man stepped out. Trooper Hinen explained to the driver why he had been pulled over and obtained the driver's license and other required commercial vehicle documents. Trooper Hinen needed practice contacting dispatch and requesting driver's license and wants checks, so he had it.

Wouldn't you know it? What was supposed to be a short, simple, red light warning turned into a can of worms. The driver had a suspended driver's license, warrants for unpaid tickets, and an altered Driver's Log Book. We arrested the driver, called for a tow truck, and had just started on the Vehicle Impound Sheet (a lengthy document required anytime you separate a driver from his vehicle). To add fuel to our flames, dispatch called and advised that a traffic accident on State Route 289 was ours. The deputy would stand by at the accident until we arrived. Damn!

A Winnemucca police officer agreed to help us out with our current situation. He would wait for the tow truck, transport our prisoner to the jail, and put him in holding until we could get there and complete the booking process. Off we headed for the wreck.

We arrived at the property damage accident at 0043 hours. It was a minor, single-vehicle accident and occurred when the driver, a gorgeous young woman about Trooper Hinen's age, drove right past the I-80 eastbound on-ramp and continued on SR 289 until she ran out of pavement and failed to negotiate a hard, left turn.

Watching Trooper Hinen converse with this pretty little gal was almost too much to bear. "Are you hurt? Are you sure you're not hurt? Is there anything I can do for you?" Oh, brother! This young trooper was single, and you would have thought it was love at first sight.

I smelled the odor of alcohol about the young woman and noticed a few physical symptoms of drinking. She seemed unsteady on her feet, her words were slightly slurred, and she seemed a little confused. Alcohol could also explain why she drove right past a big green sign with a directional arrow that read, Interstate 80 Eastbound.

Before the days of the PBT (Preliminary Breath Test) machines, which all officers now carry, determining a person's level of intoxication could be difficult. If they were not falling down drunk, it really did take time and experience to learn to sniff out a DUI. When I recall my first days, I can think of several I let go who should have gone to jail.

I asked Trooper Hinen, "Do you think you should give her a field sobriety test?"

"Oh, I don't think she's DUI," he said.

"Oh, I think she might be," I said.

"Really, do you think so?"

"I think we need to test her and find out."

"Well, okay."

Trooper Hinen ran the young woman through a series of tests, just like he learned and practiced in the academy. He did a great job administering the test for the first time. She didn't perform horribly, but she could have done better. I asked Trooper Hinen if he thought she was under the influence, and he said, "I'm not sure, but I really hope she isn't."

He asked what I thought, and I told him, "The young woman needs to be arrested for DUI and taken to jail."

He looked like a little kid who had just had his balloon popped. His enthusiasm for the new job diminished significantly in seconds.

We cuffed her up, waited for the tow truck, and off to the jail we went to book both of our prisoners. By the time we finished a legal breath test, booked both prisoners, and filled out jail paperwork, it was around 4:00 a.m. Then we had to return to our office and do more required paperwork before we could go home.

Trooper Hinen was riding in my car, and I had to drive him eight miles out of town to his residence. The sun was up, birds were chirping their morning songs, and as we pulled into his driveway I handed him the microphone so he could go off duty with our dispatch center.

After he received his off-duty time from dispatch, Trooper Hinen looked at me and asked, "Would you like to come in? I'll cook you breakfast!"

"I think we should pull the trucker over and give him a warning!" I said in a sarcastic, mocking tone. "No thank you, Trooper Hinen. Just get your ass out of my car so I can go home!"

I'll Be Right with You

I worked the road for thirteen years as a state trooper before promoting to sergeant and then lieutenant. Altogether, I estimate I made over thirty thousand traffic stops. People often ask me to describe my most memorable traffic stop, and the following story stands out as one of my favorites.

I didn't like wearing winter coats. They were bulky, cumbersome, and restrictive. During the winter months, the heater kept my office (the inside of my patrol car) nice and toasty. Most traffic stops lasted roughly ten minutes, so a coat wasn't needed unless I was out in the cold for an unusually extended period of time.

On the first approach to a violator's vehicle, an officer's senses are heightened more than any other time during the stop. This is the time when seeing the driver's hands, assessing their actions and demeanor, and being concerned for your personal welfare are critical. I always felt much safer on a traffic stop not having a restrictive coat getting in the way should gunfire or a physical confrontation take place.

The memorable traffic stop occurred one cold January morning on I-80 west of Winnemucca. While running stationary radar at the Rose Creek Interchange, I clocked a cute, little, sports car at 87 in a 55 mile-per-hour zone. Thirty-two miles per hour over the posted limit is a good catch. The driver saw me and slowed down way too late.

Every day, my "routine" traffic stops were the same: stop the car, approach cautiously, introduce myself, explain the reason for pulling the driver over, and get the documentation I needed. I would advise the driver to remain seated as I completed a citation. I would return to my patrol car, run wants and warrants through the National Crime Information Center (NCIC) and fill out the traffic citation. Citations were completed with a pen, not with the scanners and bar codes of today.

When I returned to the driver's window, I gave the same explanation every time: "You have received a citation for (whatever violation), your bail is (so many) dollars, with an appearance date in the nearest justice court. If you don't wish to appear, the posted dollar amount can be mailed to the justice court before the appearance date. Your signature is required on the citation as a promise to appear in court. If you choose not to appear, your options are listed on the back side of your copy. Your signature is required on the citation, but it is not an admission of guilt."

After stopping the sports car on I-80, I approached the driver's door. The two-seat car was occupied by a male driver and a female passenger. Everything went according to plan until I tried to issue the citation and obtain the driver's signature. The driver was clearly upset and kept interrupting me. As mentioned earlier, it was freezing and the guy who hates coats was not wearing one. Recognizing that I was freezing when I asked for his signature on the citation, the driver said, "I don't sign anything until I've read it over."

I handed the driver my ticket book and stood outside his window as he slowly and deliberately read the entire document aloud from top to bottom, which took several minutes. Shaking from the cold with a runny nose and pink cheeks, I asked the driver to sign the citation. He said, "I think I need to read it again!" His wife found this very amusing and smiled at her husband's brilliance and daring.

"That's fine," I told them. "You keep my ticket book while you read the citation again. Take your time. Make sure you understand what it says. I'll be in my patrol car, so honk your horn when you have signed the citation."

It was pure delight to return my frozen body to the comfort of my heated patrol car. I had barely sat down when I heard the horn sound. Now that I wasn't freezing outside his door, the man was in a big hurry to leave. I could see him looking at me in his rearview mirror. Holding my index finger up where he could see it, I motioned that I'd be with him in a few minutes. He wasn't likely to risk a trip to jail by driving off with my ticket book.

After a few minutes, the driver laid on his horn. I picked up my public address microphone, turned the loud speaker to high, and said, "I will be right with you!" Several minutes passed before another lengthy honk broke the silence. Using the speaker again, I said, "I will be right there!"

A few minutes later, I finally strolled up to the driver's door. The wife was laughing and smiling. She knew what her husband had done, and what I had so professionally and politely done back to him. The poor man was fuming. With all the patience in the world, I asked, "Are you ready to go or do you need more time?"

Knowing I had tortured this poor driver by putting him in timeout, I handed him his copy of the ticket and let him leave. I returned to my patrol car and sat there smiling and chuckling for the longest time before getting back on the highway to find another one.

Trained Attack Dogs

One could always count on winter setting in northern Nevada by Halloween, and the year of 1982 wasn't any different. The evening of October 25th was cold with gusting winds. The rain had turned to snow as soon as the sun went down, and the temperature dropped by twenty degrees.

At 1924 hours, on I-80 eastbound near the town of Lovelock, a Pershing County deputy stopped a black Mercedes sedan with California license plates. I don't recall why the deputy had stopped it, but when he walked up to the vehicle, the driver stepped on the gas and sped away. The deputy ran back to his patrol vehicle, a full-size Chevy Suburban, and took off in pursuit. From this little bit of information, you have to know there is no way a Suburban is going to keep up with a Mercedes, let alone catch it. The Mercedes was being driven by a middle-aged white male, accompanied by a white female of similar age.

I was working nights in the Winnemucca area, sixty miles east of where the pursuit began. Dispatch advised me of the active pursuit, so I headed west on I-80 towards Lovelock. I found a nice spot in the median, near the Humboldt-Pershing county line, where I had a good view of approaching traffic to the west. After a few minutes, I was joined by Nevada Division of Investigation Detective Rick Cornish. A Marine and Vietnam veteran, Rick was working that evening and had heard the radio traffic. Since I was the only trooper working for a hundred miles in either direction, he came to assist.

Rick was a great guy, an experienced cop who swaggered a little when he walked and did a near perfect imitation of John Wayne that would leave you in stitches. We turned off our headlights, monitored the pursuit (if you could call it that as the deputy lost sight of the Mercedes' tail lights soon after it began) and waited for them to arrive.

And here it came. Miles away in the distance we saw only one set of headlights and flashing emergency lights coming our way. As the pursuit got closer, we started getting ready to join the chase. The deputy reached our location and shot past us. But no black Mercedes sedan had come our way.

The deputy turned around and pulled into the median so we could devise a plan. There were four interchanges with off-ramps in the thirty miles of interstate between us and where the deputy last saw the car. The good thing was that none of these off-ramps, located in the middle of America's Great Basin Desert, went anywhere. We decided to leapfrog back west and check each off-ramp that the Mercedes could have exited on.

I would take the first exit, Rick the second, and the deputy the third. I didn't find any sign of them at the first, so I leapfrogged to the fourth interchange called Humboldt House. At the bottom of the off-ramp, I saw a bright, shiny, new rim gouge in the pavement of the intersecting highway. The rim gouge had not been there the night before.

When troopers work their beats daily, they know the highways they patrol intimately. I could come back to work after a week's vacation and know where every wreck had occurred since I had been gone, just from the new tire marks. A rim gouge is left when a tire goes flat, and the driver continues to drive on it.

This particular gouge began on the eastbound off-ramp, continued under the overpass, made a hard right turn onto another roadway, and stopped right on the north side of the highway at the rear of a black Mercedes sedan with California plates. The tire had gone flat as the driver took the hard left at the bottom of the ramp at a high rate of speed. Surprisingly, this action didn't result in a rollover. The driver was certainly pushing the car past its limits.

The engine was running, the headlights were on, both doors were wide open, and two sets of footprints (one large, one small) headed out into the desert in the new snow. I pulled up with my emergency lights activated, headlights pointed toward the desert, and scanned the area with my 100,000 candlepower spotlight. There were no visible signs of anyone.

I grabbed my public address system microphone and said, "This is the state police. Walk toward the light with your hands in the air."

I waited, but there was no response.

Minutes later, Detective Cornish pulled up in his unmarked car. I quickly filled him in on the situation. Rick walked over to my patrol car, picked up the public address microphone which I had left dangling out of the car window, and said, "This is the police. We have trained attack dogs on their way to this location. When we turn these attack dogs loose, we cannot be responsible for their actions, or for any injuries you are sure to incur. I repeat, this is the police and we have trained attack dogs on their way to this location. When we turn these attack dogs loose, we cannot be responsible for their actions, or for any injuries you are sure to incur."

With a satisfied look on his face, Rick put the microphone down and looked at me.

"We have trained attack dogs?" I asked.

"No," he replied.

"Is someone else bringing trained attack dogs here?"

"No."

"Then where in the hell did you come up with that one?"

"I saw it in a movie once."

"Did it work?"

He shook his head and said, "No. No, it didn't."

It's a good thing tears are salty and don't freeze easily, because we laughed until we couldn't see. It didn't work this time either. Hearing us laugh so hard when we were looking for bad guys probably scared the heck out of them. No one wants to get caught by crazy officers.

The deputy arrived shortly after and told us the Mercedes had been reported stolen in California. Since it was the deputy's county and his pursuit, we asked him what he wanted to do.

"Well, it's too damn nasty out to search for crooks. And we don't even know how bad of crooks they are. We couldn't easily round up anyone else on short notice to help, so I say we tow the car and go home."

"Okey dokey," I said. "These folks are going to spend one miserable night outdoors."

While the deputy waited for the tow truck, I went to the one and only ranch house within three miles of there and told the owners what had occurred. I was kind of hoping these crooks would show up there, but they might have known better than walking up to a Nevada ranch house in the middle of the night. That is a good way to end up dead!

So, they got away. But you have to look at the bright side. Crooks breed and raise little crooks. If you catch them all before they have little ones, who are we going to have to chase around in the future? It's job security!

This Corvette is the Coolest

My good friend Trooper Doug Darlington and I were both working I-80 late one summer morning. Trooper Darlington called on the radio and said he was trying to catch up to a yellow Corvette west of Winnemucca. He estimated the car's speed at over 120 miles per hour before he'd lost sight of it.

I headed west to intercept the Corvette. As I traveled around Winnemucca on I-80, I saw the yellow Corvette take the off-ramp into town. The driver slowed, and I caught up to it on Winnemucca Blvd. I activated the overhead emergency lights and advised Trooper Darlington that I had found his speeder. The Corvette pulled into a convenience store parking lot and stopped.

I contacted the driver, a young man, and told him I was holding him for another trooper who would be along soon. Minutes later, Trooper Darlington arrived. He told the young man he'd estimated his speed at over 120 miles per hour in a 55-mph zone. Trooper Darlington hadn't been able to get a radar reading on the Corvette, so he told the young man that he'd cite him for 90 in a 55-mph zone if he admitted how fast he'd been going. The man said he'd been driving over 130 mph.

While Trooper Darlington wrote out the ticket, we spoke with the young man about his car and his trip. He was polite and told us this was the coolest car he'd ever owned. It went much faster than 130 mph and handled like a dream. Trooper Darlington and I cleared from the traffic stop and left the young man at the convenience store.

Two hours later, the Oregon State Police contacted us about the young man we had ticketed earlier. The young man was operating his

Corvette at a high rate of speed and lost control while pulling out to pass another vehicle traveling in the same direction. Oregon State Police arrived at the accident scene twenty-two miles north of the Nevada-Oregon state line on US 95. The fiberglass car had left the roadway and disintegrated as it rolled and tumbled across the desert. Scattered among the debris was the citation Trooper Darlington had issued earlier that day.

The young man had picked up a six pack of beer at the same convenience store in Winnemucca after we left him. We calculated the time and distance he had traveled since our last contact in Winnemucca and showed that he'd averaged over 100 mph. Including the time it took him to buy the beer and get through town, we figured he'd been traveling at 110 to 120 mph—but this time on a rural, two-lane highway.

At 120 mph, a vehicle travels at 162 feet (over half the length of a football field) every second. There is little room for error when traveling that fast. Carelessness cost this young man his life.

Who Canceled the Ambulance?

I loved my career. Every day, with a few exceptions, I enthusiastically dressed in my French blue uniform and went out my front door in search of adventure. While bad days were few and far between, when I did have one, it was really bad.

State troopers spend a substantial amount of time responding to, mitigating, investigating, and documenting motor vehicle accidents. Accidents which occur on the open highway quite often result in serious, sometimes fatal injuries to occupants due to the high vehicle speeds traveled. It's a common occurrence, and troopers do get used to working these situations.

When working a fatal accident scene, it's a good thing the trooper is kept busy performing required tasks. It helps to put aside the tragedy that has just taken place. It's sad of course, but it's not usually something that we would dwell on or fret over. It's just the way things are.

But every once in a while, the sadness of one of those tragedies would hit home. Perhaps it was a child that reminded you of your own. Or it was someone you happened to know, or a family member of a close friend. Sometimes you didn't know or understand why one event could bother you more than the next.

On a beautiful, bright, sunny mid-morning, I was dispatched to a one-car rollover accident on I-80 westbound at the West Winnemucca Interchange. I happened to be right in town when the call came and arrived on scene within two minutes of notification.

The scene was not pretty upon arrival. A car was visible off the west roadway edge and exhibited extensive rollover damage. It was apparent that this vehicle had rolled multiple times before coming to rest on its top. Lying next to a marker post just off the west roadway edge was a young male adult. It was very apparent that he had been ejected during the violent rollover and had struck his head against a steel post. Without going into any more detail, I will simply say the young man's death was immediate.

Lying on the pavement and partially in the travel lane was a very beautiful young adult woman. This young woman had severe head injuries, but was still alive. All my attention was focused on her, yet sadly there was nothing I could do to save her. All I could do was hold her hand, sit there and watch her die.

I was an EMT and had been to enough of these events to know that it wouldn't be long until she expired. After a few minutes that seemed like an eternity, the young woman died. This was one of the most difficult things I have ever had to see. A young beautiful woman, someone's daughter, the deceased young man's new bride, dying before my eyes and not a thing could be done to save her. It was a very helpless feeling and very sad for me, a trooper who was used to arriving at accident scenes and helping victims.

A funny thing about Nevada law is that only a coroner or physician can legally pronounce death. Even if a body is missing its head and has been that way for a year, the person is not officially dead until the coroner says so. Most Nevada counties have no official Coroner's Office, so the sheriff's deputies are trained to perform that task.

Since we were right on the edge of town, Humboldt County Sheriff's Deputy and Coroner Dan Jones arrived on scene a few minutes after the young woman's last breath. Deputy Jones had only been a deputy for a short time. Prior to his employment in Nevada, he'd retired as a Los Angeles Fireman/Paramedic. Deputy Jones had seen more severe accidents than I had, and I had seen plenty. Deputy Jones checked both accident victims and pronounced them deceased.

At the time, our local Humboldt County ambulance service was entirely comprised of volunteers. That meant that when notified of a call, they had to proceed from their homes or businesses to the Ambulance Barn, wait for a crew, and fire up the ambulance before departure. Rural state troopers almost always beat the ambulance to an accident scene. We would administer first aid with the horrible "worst aid kits" the state of Nevada could possibly provide. Then we would impatiently wait for help to arrive. When help finally did show up, they were very skilled and dedicated to their part-time profession.

In this particular case, I had not heard the ambulance come on duty, meaning they had not yet left the ambulance barn. I contacted Elko NHP Dispatch and asked her to cancel the ambulance.

There is a ton of work to be done at the scene of a fatal car wreck: tend to any injured victims, arrange for the transport of the deceased, photograph the scene, locate evidence, diagram the scene, inspect vehicles, arrange for towing, and re-open any closed portions of the roadway. I was at the scene for about two hours when I advised NHP Elko Dispatch that I was 10-8 (clear) from the scene and 10-76 (en route) to the office. Dispatch advised that I 10-5 (meet with) the emergency room doctor at Humboldt General Hospital. I proceeded to the hospital, parked outside of the emergency room, and walked through the sliding doors.

I knew all the local doctors, but this one I hadn't seen before. He must have been one of the substitute doctors that came from somewhere else to work the emergency room under contract.

As I approached the doctor, he asked in a curt voice, "Are you the trooper who was at the scene of the bad car wreck?" I told him that I was, and he screamed, "Who the hell do you think you are canceling an ambulance?

Of all the days of my career to pick to scream at me, this was not the day. I immediately saw red, and though I don't remember everything I said, I do remember backing that little asshole up against the wall with my finger in his chest and screaming back at him.

"Who the hell do you think *you* are? You sit in your pretty, sterile emergency room and think you're going to call the shots from three miles away? They were dead! Don't want to take my word for it? How about I have a twenty-five-year Los Angeles fireman and paramedic come explain it to you. He's seen more dead bodies than you have ever thought of seeing. If that young woman was ejected from her car and landed on your operating table, you still couldn't have saved her!"

I then promptly turned around and walked out. I waited days for the formal complaint to hit my sergeant's desk, but it never came. I guess the doctor was a few pegs shorter and didn't have the heart to go after me again.

The story of this tragic accident went as follows. The young woman was a US Army sergeant, and the young man an Army private. They were married the week before at their base at Ft. Ord, California and decided to make a quick five-day trip to her parent's house in Indiana. They took turns driving cross-country for a day and a half to get there. After visiting for two days, they were driving back when the young woman fell asleep, drove off the road, overcorrected, and overturned. Inside the car were two speeding citations they had received on their way back east. They were driving day and night and they were driving fast. A deadly combination and a fatal mistake.

You Don't Say

"6144 Elko."

"6144."

"We have a report of shots fired at a commercial vehicle on US 95, thirty-one miles north of Winnemucca. The driver was not hit by gunfire, but was beaten, robbed and reported to have a broken leg. Winnemucca ambulance will be en route."

"10-4 Elko, 10-76."

Wow, I thought. That's a crazy call, especially on such a cold, snowy, miserable, winter morning. Whoever perpetrated this crime surely wasn't a fair weather bad guy. It sounded more like a desperate criminal or an angry acquaintance.

When I arrived, a red cab-over International tractor and semi-trailer were parked off the east roadway edge (cab-over tractors had a flat front and have disappeared from America's highways). Not having any clue what had actually happened, I searched the area a few minutes for any sign of danger before I stepped out of my car. For all I knew the perpetrator was still armed and in the immediate area.

I walked to the front of the commercial vehicle through a few inches of fresh snow and found several good Samaritans standing around a man lying on the ground. He had been wrapped in blankets for protection from the snow and for treatment of possible shock. I pulled back the blanket and immediately noticed a disfigured lower leg. I asked the driver what happened, and he told the following story.

He was driving northbound when at least four bullets struck his front windshield. A man with a rifle was standing in the road in front of him and motioning him to the shoulder, so he pulled over and stopped. The man gestured for him to get out, so he climbed down and met the man in front of the tractor. The assailant gave a kick to the side of his lower leg, breaking it. Then the man robbed him of $1,500 in cash which belonged to his company and fled.

I asked what the assailant was driving when he left. The driver told me he never saw a vehicle and didn't see the man leave. He was in severe pain and remained on the ground until motorists stopped and wrapped him in a blanket.

An armed assailant, in a snowstorm, in the middle of the desert, with no apparent means of transportation, was taking shots at the windshield of a northbound commercial vehicle. At sixty miles an hour the assailant supposedly motioned for the driver to stop and he did. I would have mashed the accelerator to the floor and continued on. There was obviously damage to the windshield. The man was clearly lying in the snow with a broken leg. Something happened, but what?

I turned my attention to the windshield supposedly filled with bullet holes. A bullet that strikes and penetrates a hard object, like a windshield, will leave a very distinctive mark. If the bullet was shot perpendicular to the glass, the hole will be round and similar in size to the caliber of the bullet. These breaks were not even close to what a bullet hole should look like. Instead they looked like strike marks in the glass made by a short steel pipe I found lying in the snow in front of the truck.

Cab-over tractors had a narrow bumper with step holes. Handles were built into the front, under the windows, to use when washing the windshields. I found shoe marks in the snow and grime on the top of the bumper. One mark continued a short distance down the front of the bumper. Clearly, someone had stood on top of the icy bumper and slipped off.

I brought these inconsistencies to the attention of the driver, but he wasn't budging from his story of being shot at and robbed. The volunteer ambulance had not arrived yet, so I had several minutes to cast doubt on his fable. Finally, he admitted that he had made up the entire story. The broken leg happened when he stepped onto the top of the skinny, icy bumper to hit the windshield with his tire iron and fell. My next question was obvious. Why did he feel the need to dream up such an incredibly unbelievable story in the first place?

It turned out the story was invented to cover his employer's missing $1,500. Did the boss' money fall out of the driver's pocket after he cashed the check? No. Did he stop at one of Winnemucca's casinos and lose it at the gaming tables? No. Did he drink it away? No. Then where did the money go? Well, it turns out the driver spent the preceding night at one of Winnemucca's four legal brothels. Fifteen hundred dollars gone, but what a time he must have had.

Like most things in life, if you want to dance, you must pay the band. If you want to spend an entire night at a Nevada brothel using your boss' money meant for fuel, you had better make up a very believable story you can sell to the cops.

It is a crime in Nevada to fabricate and relate such a bogus story to an officer. Either filing a false crime report or obstructing and delaying a law enforcement officer in the performance of their duties will work. The volunteer ambulance arrived right after I issued the driver a citation for the latter crime. Off he went in the ambulance, never to be seen by me again. Obviously, he pled guilty.

Rated X

In the Academy, troopers told a few stories about catching people in compromising positions while on patrol. Most of the stories were interesting and humorous, while others just made you shake your head. After patrolling both days and nights for several years, I had never encountered any sexual escapades. Not until one hot summer afternoon.

While on patrol on I-80, I noticed a car traveling eastbound that caught my eye. What distinguished this car from the hundreds of others that had passed me that day? Well, this two-door sedan had two people in one seat. The driver's seat!

I crossed over the median at the first opportunity and caught up to the car. A young woman was sitting on the driver's lap and facing the rear of the car. Sure enough, what I thought was happening, was happening at sixty miles per hour!

I positioned my patrol car directly behind the sedan with red and blue lights flashing. Try to imagine the young woman's surprise when she finally noticed my patrol car directly behind her. She returned to the passenger seat so fast it's a wonder no injuries were incurred!

The driver pulled over immediately. I walked up to the sedan and the young man rolled the window down. He had a sheepish, "hand in the cookie jar" expression on his face. They were a fine-looking, obviously happy, young couple who were beyond embarrassed at being discovered. The poor young woman sat with her face buried in her hands.

"What on earth are you doing making love while driving down the highway at sixty mph?" I asked.

"We're on our honeymoon," the young man replied. "I guess that wasn't such a good idea."

"Not such a good idea? I understand you were just married, but that is exactly the reason God created rest areas. One of which you passed twenty miles ago. Another is seven miles ahead. Then again, it's still daylight and you could get arrested there as well!"

One of the main reasons for traffic enforcement is to gain voluntary compliance in the future. I checked the required driving documents, and everything appeared in order. Next, I would have to decide whether to issue the love-struck honeymooners a citation or let them go with a warning.

I was pretty sure the young couple would refrain from committing this heinous crime in the future. Even if the young man was game for another go, I was willing to bet this young woman wouldn't leave her seat again, even if asked nicely. I let them go with a warning.

A traffic stop I will never forget. A traffic stop this young couple will never forget. A traffic stop this couple most likely will not tell their grandchildren.

The Longest Train Ride

One of my very best friends in this world is named Dennis Mastin. He is the kindest man you could ever hope to meet, the sort of guy who would give you the shirt off his back. I often teased Dennis about collecting people, one of his favorite pastimes. Anyone down on their luck, with a sad story, ended up living in his basement, often accompanied by their spouses, kids and dogs. Dennis worked hard as a railroader to feed and house these folks, many of whom slept in each day, with no intention of finding a job. Eventually, he would grow tired of their lame excuses and lies, and trade them in for a new set.

Dennis was a conductor for the Union Pacific Railroad. I had always been intrigued by trains and relished the thought of riding a locomotive. Dennis was interested in my profession as a patrolman and asked to ride along with me sometime. The only problem was that neither of us was allowed to carry an unauthorized passenger while at work. I was always a stickler for following the rules, but this time we both decided to bend the rules and take each other to work for a day.

One evening, I picked up Dennis in my patrol car. We stopped a few cars, wrote a few citations, and handled a minor traffic accident. After a relatively uneventful night, I dropped my friend off at his home.

My turn to go to work with Dennis came several months later. Dennis' normal route crossed northern Nevada from west to east. The train ride from Winnemucca to the city of Elko would take three to four hours. Dennis had a car in Elko he needed me to drive back to Winnemucca. Railroad locomotives are massive and powerful. I was really looking forward to boarding the train.

Dennis picked me up at my home and off we drove to the train yard. After he completed some paperwork, it was time to climb on the engine and head for Elko. As Dennis introduced me to the engineer, he turned around in his big chair and my heart sank. His name was Sam, and I had arrested him for driving under the influence a year or so before. My job was never personal, and I certainly had no hard feelings for him. Sam, on the other hand, did not like me at all.

Hate is probably a better descriptive word for Sam's feelings toward me. When I arrested Sam, the law required him to submit to a chemical test to determine the alcohol content of his blood. At that time, a person could choose between a blood test, a breath test, or a urine test (no longer an option). Sam chose a urine test. Performed at the hospital, the arrestee urinates into a container in the presence of the officer. After thirty minutes of babysitting the drunk and pouring water down them, they are required to fill a second container. Hoping they can pee again is a real drag.

With Sam under arrest, searched and handcuffed, and belted into my patrol car, we headed for Humboldt General Hospital. I filled out the required paperwork and accompanied Sam into the toilet. Without going into detail, this part of the test was the worst. Sam finished and then handed me the container. It is really weird standing next to another man in a restroom hoping he can pee. If the arrestee fails to urinate again in thirty minutes, the test is incomplete and not admissible in court.

During these thirty minutes, it is advantageous to have the arrestee drink as much water as possible, which I did. Having nothing to say, Sam gave me the evil eye the whole time. Thirty minutes finally passed, and it was time for Sam to produce a second sample. While filling the container, Sam leaned over and spit water he had been holding in his mouth into the cup. No wonder he had nothing to say.

Sam failed the test and lost his driving privileges for six months. I took him to jail, booked him, and never saw him again until climbing aboard the engine. In reality, I did Sam a favor because he never drank another drop of alcohol.

So, the fun trip on the train began. Every second Sam wasn't looking out the train window, he was glaring at me. And since the train is on a track, the engineer seldom has to look outside. It's not like he has to steer the darn thing.

I told Dennis how Sam and I met, and he became uncomfortable about the situation as well. Dennis worried that Sam might rat him out for bringing me on the train. Hours later, we pulled into the Elko railroad yard. It was a very long, tense, quiet, dreadful trip.

Sam never said a word regarding my unauthorized ride, but he did express his dislike for me to Dennis every chance he got. Years later, after I retired from the Nevada Highway Patrol, I ran for sheriff of Humboldt County. Sam told Dennis he voted for me even though he disliked me. I lost the election by sixty-nine votes. Sam died, and I never got the chance to thank him for his vote, nor for turning what should have been a fun night into the longest train ride ever.

What a Mess

"Good morning, Trooper Raabe," my cheerful dispatcher said as I awoke from a sound sleep. "We have a report of a 10-50 Paul (property damage accident) involving a commercial vehicle, on I-80 eastbound, twenty-five miles west of Winnemucca. Your 10-41 (on-duty time) is 0409 hours."

It was June 14, 1986, sunrise was an hour and twenty minutes away, and it looked like it was going to be a beautiful summer day. I threw on my uniform, strapped on my gun belt, and fired up my patrol car. Since it was reported as a property damage accident, with no reported injuries, I made a quick pit stop at a convenience store to grab a cup of coffee and some orange juice to go.

I didn't run code 3 (lights and sirens), but I still made good time. As I headed that direction, I noticed there was no traffic on the eastbound side of I-80. My property damage accident must be blocking the highway, I presumed. Three miles east of the accident scene, dispatch called.

"6144 Elko, your 10-50 Paul is now reported as a 10-50 Frank times two (double fatality), one subject critical, eastbound lanes blocked."

Within a mile of the accident scene, I could see numerous red fuses burning on the east side of the interstate, followed by a sea of stationary headlights stretching out toward the west. Vehicles, mostly trucks, were crossing the median one at a time to avoid the accident and the delay. First order of business was to put an end to that. I didn't need another accident to add to the mess and what a mess it was!

101

I contacted two drivers by CB radio, and they agreed to move their trucks and block the median crossover for me.

The remnants of vehicle number 1 (V1), a *Wheaton Van Lines* tractor with the trailer still attached, was lying on its right side and blocking both eastbound lanes of I-80. The entire cab of V1 was literally gone from the frame and chassis. Another tractor-trailer, *Munson Transportation* or vehicle number 5 (V5), was lying on its left side, also blocking the eastbound lanes. The entire cab of V1, which had been scraped off, was fused to the front and top of the cab of V5.

Another tractor-trailer, a *Bekin's Van Lines* or vehicle number 3 (V3), was upright, in the median portion of the highway, facing east. Another tractor-trailer, a *Packerland Transport* or vehicle number 4 (V4), was upright in the median, east of V3, facing east. A truck load of someone's household belongings, being moved by Wheaton Van Lines were scattered everywhere.

My first concern after arranging for traffic control was to check on the status of every person involved. Two men and a woman involved in the accident were not injured. One of the truck drivers, Richard Ross, confirmed the information dispatch had just given to me, but added that a co-driver was missing.

Mr. Ross led me to a man lying in the median. I checked him for signs of life and there weren't any. His body was nowhere close to any involved vehicle. I had worked hundreds of accidents and my experience told me that it didn't make sense for him to land so far away. The man was beyond help, so I moved on.

Mr. Ross led me to the body of a man who had been partially ejected from the cab of V1 and no visible signs of life were detected. We then continued on to the injured driver of V5. The man was being attended to. He had been entirely ejected out of the front windshield of his tractor and came to rest on the roadway. His injuries were severe, but he appeared stable. I spoke with him, and he asked about his co-driver who had been in the sleeper compartment of his tractor (V5). No one had seen or heard from him. Mr. Ross said he had hollered into the cab of V5, but there was no answer. There was so much twisted, sharp metal that he didn't try to get inside.

I was able to crawl into the wreckage and locate the missing co-driver in the sleeper compartment. He had received fatal injuries and was wrapped up in the metal.

At 0551 hours, I returned to my patrol car to inform dispatch of the situation. I asked her to call out the cavalry and then check the location of the responding ambulance, so I could direct it in. I was going to need lots of help. Eastbound traffic had been completely stopped since the accident occurred and was backed up for miles. I was going to need traffic control, a TAR (Traffic Accident Reconstruction expert) on scene to assist me with the investigation, a coroner, a funeral home to transport the deceased, troopers to help with cleanup and towing, and a sergeant.

I tended to the injured driver until we could get him shipped off to the hospital. Within forty minutes, the ambulance, a sergeant, and four other troopers had arrived. Sergeant Glen Jewett took charge of traffic control at the scene and supervised clean up and towing operations. Trooper Don Smith dealt with the giant traffic mess west of the accident scene. Trooper Chuck Stamey was our photographer, obtained witness statements from the two drivers still alive at the scene, and started the long process of gathering all the driver's licenses, vehicle registrations (including trailers), insurance information, bills of lading, and then documenting all the information. Pershing County Sheriff Kay MacIntosh performed coroner duties and took possession of the deceased. Highway Patrol Corporal Bill Souza was a TAR, and he and I worked as a team to locate and document evidence.

An accident scene is like a crime scene in that every piece of evidence plays a role in determining what happened. Figuring it all out would come later. Right now, locating, identifying, and recording the evidence were the most important tasks.

Each one of the vehicles involved had eighteen wheels. Tire marks, rim gouges, and scratches where metal parts slid across the pavement were everywhere. Every dent, missing vehicle part, paint transfer, impression, and resting body tells the story of how each vehicle collided with the other, where, and the path they took afterward.

We located the dead man in the median and took some measurements. He was identified as the co-driver of the Wheaton Vans Lines, V1. It did not make any sense for him to be located so far west of where the collision between his vehicle and V5 took place. The only part of his body that had sustained any injury was the left side of his head. Both drivers belonging to the two tractor-trailers which remained upright were still at the scene. Both drivers had been asked what happened, but neither mentioned seeing this man, nor how he came to be where he was. His body was located just to the left of the tire tracks left in the dirt by V3.

Corporal Souza walked to the front of V3, a white 1982 Kenworth cabover tractor. The left headlight frame was broken, and there was a small indentation and broken fiberglass just below it. A closer look revealed facial hairs (whiskers) imbedded in the fiberglass. The dead driver in the median had been hit and killed by V3.

Corporal Souza and I located the driver of V3 and asked him if he remembered seeing or hitting anyone. The driver hung his head and speaking to his chest said, "Yes, I saw him running. He was trying to get out of the way, but he didn't make it."

This driver did nothing wrong, but it would have been nice if he had shared that information with us an hour or two earlier.

It took hours to take measurements, get the vehicles removed, and the debris and household belongings cleaned up. A small convoy of Marines stopped and helped with the clean up. The household belongings were mostly trash and were taken to the tow yard for the owners to pick through later.

We finished at the scene around noon. It had been a long day. Completing reports, drawing diagrams of the scene, figuring out how this accident occurred and the sequence of events, would take at least a week.

Corporal Souza and I spent most of the next day playing with trucks. We used toy semi-trucks, similar to those involved, and recreated the accident scene using masking tape on the floor of the Winnemucca highway patrol office. Measurements were reduced in size to the scale of the toy trucks. We built the lanes of I-80 eastbound and recreated pertinent roadway marks, fluid trails from ruptured tanks, locations of large debris, and plotted the direction each vehicle took to their final position of rest.

It took us hours to review the previous day's documents, witness statements, examine roadway marks and contact damage to each of the commercial vehicles involved. With perseverance, debate, sore knees, getting strange looks from visitors, and Corporal Souza having to listen to me make occasional putt-putt sounds as I moved the trucks around, we finally figured it out.

The *Wheaton Van Lines*, V1, had been traveling eastbound at a high rate of speed. A witness the truck had passed minutes before the accident estimated his speed at eighty-five to ninety miles per hour. The driver was not paying attention or fell asleep, most likely the latter, and his tractor-trailer left the pavement into the soft dirt of the median. The driver overcorrected, and the tractor-trailer regained the roadway. Additional oversteering, the grade of the median, and V1's momentum caused it to overturn on its left side. It came to rest blocking the entire eastbound paved portion of the highway at an angle.

At that point, the entire situation stabilized and technically the first accident was over. The driver, condition and actions unknown, stayed inside the overturned tractor, while the co-driver got out. The co-driver pedestrian (P2) walked back toward oncoming traffic to warn them of the hazard.

Along came three tractor-trailers with no clue about what lay before them. *Bekins Van Lines* (V3) and *Packerland Transport* (V4) were traveling beside each other while *Munson Transportation* (V5) was behind them. Wheaton Van Lines (V1) lay on its side and was blocking the highway at such an angle that the only way to avoid it was to steer to the left and drive into the median.

Pedestrian #2 saw that neither vehicle was going to be able to stop and his only route of escape was into the median as well. V3 and V4 sideswiped each other as they left the roadway into the dirt median. P2, running in the soft dirt to get away, came within a foot of escaping, but was struck and killed by the left front of V3.

When V3 and V4 left the pavement, into the dirt median, it created a giant cloud of dust totally obscuring the driver of V5's vision. Without any time to react or brake, V5 drove into the top of V1's overturned trailer, sheering off the front third of the trailer and the cab of the tractor in its entirety. This collision resulted in the deaths of Driver #1, the co-driver in the sleeper birth of V5, and the ejection and severe injuries to the driver of V5.

I was later called to a deposition conducted by the different attorneys representing all parties involved. I was questioned for hours, but my report was wrapped tight, and no one disputed my findings. I don't know who paid who, or how much, but you can bet it was a substantial amount.

End of the Road

We say that Nevada has four seasons: fall, winter, spring, and road construction. Keeping the construction workers safe was our job. And it's a challenging job too, as it has always been difficult to slow traffic in construction zones. Sometimes there are miles of orange cones before you see an actual worker, and I think this can cause drivers to not exercise the care they should.

The Nevada Department of Transportation crews were our neighbors and friends. They run snow plows in the worst of conditions, set up traffic control when large accidents blocked the roads, and keep highways and rest areas in good condition. NDOT employees worked hard, but we would tease them about being lazy. We would tell them that their jobs were being threatened by the Japanese invention of a shovel that stands up by itself.

Another classic joke was of the NDOT employee who grew annoyed with a snail and stepped on it because he was tired of it following him around all day. The fact is, they had a dangerous job, and we didn't want them killed or injured.

One sunny, summer morning, I was working I-80 near the small town of Imlay. NHP Dispatch gave me an ATL (attempt to locate) on a four-door sedan traveling eastbound in a reckless manner. The eyewitness reported a lone woman behind the wheel.

I located the vehicle several miles west of Imlay heading toward an active construction zone. I moved into a position behind the woman and activated the overhead lights. After following a short while, I turned on the siren. With no response from the driver, I pulled into the left travel lane beside the woman's window. With lights flashing and siren screaming, the woman never looked in my direction. Driving below the posted limit, the woman ignored everything including me.

The construction zone was a mile ahead of us with traffic reduced down to a single lane. Dispatch advised NDOT that we were headed their way and would arrive at the construction zone within minutes. With little notice, NDOT workers cleared the only lane for this crazy woman. On we went at 40 mph for another ninety-five miles passing the towns of Winnemucca, Golconda and Battle Mountain. Another construction zone east of Battle Mountain had been informed, and NDOT cleared the road.

Trooper Larry Reynolds, stationed in Battle Mountain, was returning from a trip to Elko. He was the closest trooper to help and was east of my location. As this ridiculously slow pursuit progressed across northern Nevada, Trooper Reynolds and I spoke by radio and came up with a plan.

Between Battle Mountain and Elko is an interchange on State Route 306 that leads to the tiny community of Beowawe (pronounced Be-o-wow-wee). Trooper Reynolds would park his patrol car on the Beowawe Interchange overpass. By blocking the interstate, we hoped the woman would take the off-ramp and head towards Beowawe. It was the first interchange Trooper Reynolds could get to where he could help.

SR 306 led to Nowhere, USA. Beyond Beowawe is the end of pavement and miles of desert with dirt roads and sage brush. A person not familiar with this desert could spend a good part of their life finding their way back to pavement.

As the pursuit progressed southbound on SR 306, I continued in the primary position while Trooper Reynolds took the secondary position. The secondary trooper generally stays a safe distance behind, taking care of radio traffic with dispatch, coordinating with other responding officers and agencies, and planning other pursuit-ending tactics. As we proceeded south, the woman, who hadn't gone over 40 mph in one hundred miles, had increased her speed to over 90 mph and began drifting into the opposite lane on every curve. SR 306 is never busy, but I could see a head-on collision at every turn. I slowed and created distance between us, hoping the woman would slow down and stay on her side of the highway.

Keep in mind these were Trooper Reynolds' stomping grounds. I had driven this highway only once, years before, on a deer hunting trip. As I approached Beowawe, I lost sight of the violator as the vehicle disappeared around a curve. I arrived at the curve at over seventy miles per hour when Trooper Reynolds said over the radio, "Watch out for the railroad tracks."

Before finishing his sentence, my patrol car launched over a pair of tracks with an elevated crossing. I thought my Mustang would never come down. I landed at the tail end of a left curve. My pony hit hard, but I managed keep it upright and on the road. I thanked Trooper Reynolds for his warning, only wishing he would have shared that tip a bit sooner.

I caught up to the vehicle soon after the pavement turned to dirt. This remote part of our state is known as the Crescent Valley. The Cortez Mountains border the east side of the valley and are home to the Cortez Gold Mine. The woman turned left onto the road that dead-ended at the mine. Dispatch contacted the local deputy who had two of the gold mine's giant front-end loaders block the road.

Out of options, the woman made a sharp left turn to miss the loaders and drove on into the sagebrush. She lost control of the vehicle which slid broadside and became stuck in the sand. Trooper Reynolds and I approached the vehicle with caution. After determining that the woman had no weapons, we tried to speak to her. The woman didn't move, speak, or open her eyes. Her vitals appeared normal and she had no apparent injuries. We removed her from the car and laid her onto a blanket. It seemed that she had suffered some kind of a mental breakdown.

After the ambulance arrived, we sent her off to the hospital. Besides being charged with traffic offenses, I requested the hospital hold the woman for a mental health evaluation. Often, we would not learn the disposition of a case, so I don't know what became of the woman.

Every day brought something new. Some days we dealt with real criminals. Other days we dealt with sick, disturbed people.

I Can't Open the Window

Nevadans had never had a speed limit on our open highways before the federally imposed 55-mph limit. In the wide-open spaces of the American West, the federal speed limit was despised. However, no group detested it more than the Nevada Highway Patrol.

The federal government checked vehicle speeds at thirty different sites across our state four times each year. They measured what percentage of our traffic traveled above the federally posted speed limit and compliance standards. Nevada was seldom, if ever, in compliance and the federal government threatened to withhold federal highway funds. For a state like Nevada with lots of land, miles of highway, and few people, these funds are a necessity. When threatened by the loss of funds, politicians and state leaders held the highway patrol responsible for keeping drivers in compliance.

At the same time, our legislature, in their infinite wisdom, passed the "Waste of a Natural Resource" law. This allowed drivers to travel up to 70 mph in a 55-mph zone. If caught, the drivers would receive a fifteen-dollar fine and no points against their driver's license. We called this statute, the "Waste of time" law. Catching speeders was like the old saying: shooting fish in a barrel.

One morning, I was working I-80 twenty-five miles east of Winnemucca near the Pumpernickel Interchange. West of the interchange is a long, significant grade starting up the mountain towards Golconda Summit. I saw a large armored truck coming eastbound down the grade traveling well over the speed limit. I checked the truck several times on radar at 85 mph in a 55-mph zone.

I pulled the armored truck over one mile east of Pumpernickel and walked up to the driver's small, locked, armored window. A male driver opened a small port so we could converse, and asked why I had pulled him over. I asked if he knew how fast he had been going. He said he hadn't been paying attention. I informed him that I had checked his truck on radar at 85 mph and I needed to see his driver's license and vehicle registration.

The man had the documents in his hand and said, "I am not allowed to get out of this truck or open the window to give you anything. You could be a robber trying to steal our load!"

I was quite surprised that he was afraid of me as there were two more guards inside the truck, and they each had machine guns to my single pistol. It was broad daylight in the middle of the flat desert. There were no trees or rocks for miles where my fictitious accomplices could be hiding. And surely this man could not miss that I was a state trooper. I was dressed in a French blue highway patrol uniform, with a gun, badge, hat, and numerous other attachments. Not to mention the bright blue and silver highway patrol car parked behind him with the words State Trooper painted on the front fenders, the Nevada State Seal on the doors, and large overhead lights attached to the roof flashing alternating colors of red and blue.

I looked at the driver and asked, "You're kidding me, right?"

"No sir," he replied. "I'm not allowed to open any doors or exit this vehicle unless I am at a sheriff's office."

"Can't you slide the little window open and hand out your paperwork?" I asked.

"No, I may not," he said.

"Well, I guess you will have to follow me to the sheriff's office in Winnemucca where I can get the documents I need."

"I can't do that," the driver replied. "We're going to Battle Mountain."

"No sir, you are going to Winnemucca," I said. "The Humboldt County Sheriff's Office is in Winnemucca, and that is where we are going!"

"You know, I could make an exception this one time and open the window."

"Oh no! No one is breaking company rules today!" I replied. "I won't have you opening that little window where you're not supposed to!"

"It would be alright to open it this once," he said in a pathetic last attempt to get back on the road.

"No," I said. "We are going to the sheriff's office, so no one gets in trouble."

So off we went to Winnemucca. Twenty-seven miles later at the sheriff's office, the driver stepped out of his truck and received his citation.

I don't know if the driver was telling the truth about not getting out of the armored truck or opening the little window. After a story like that, there was no way I was going to let him change his mind and carry on. Besides, for me it all paid the same.

My Neck Is Broken

Often when you tell someone you are from Nevada, they think of Las Vegas. Las Vegas is warm in the winter and boiling in the summer. People are surprised to learn that winters in northern Nevada are nothing like the ones in Las Vegas. In fact, the state of Nevada has more mountain ranges than any other state in the United States with the exception of Alaska. The valleys between these mountains ranges vary from 4500 to 7000 feet in elevation. Winter storms regularly bring snow and ice to northern Nevada highways. With snow and ice come car and truck wrecks.

Early one morning, in the middle of a snow storm, an injury accident occurred on I-80. The accident was reported as a single vehicle rollover just west of the Humboldt Interchange. It occurred just west of the border between NHP Region II and III, so it would be investigated by a trooper from Lovelock. I happened to be much closer, so I was the first to arrive on scene.

Upon arrival, I noticed a four-door passenger car just off the north roadway edge. The vehicle had slid broadside off the edge of the icy pavement, overturned violently once its tires dug into the soft dirt, and then finally rolled to a rest on its wheels.

The accident involved a man, his wife, and their two teenage children. All were standing outside of the vehicle except for the woman who was still seated in the front passenger seat. The man and his children were very upset. They had some minor cuts and scratches but were otherwise uninjured. The man met me and told me his wife was injured. I went to the passenger side of the vehicle and introduced

114

myself. She was a very pretty woman, in her late-thirties, with an athletic build.

In a very calm voice, the woman said, "I am a nurse. My neck is broken. I heard it break. I felt it break and I can't move any part of my body. You need to use a backboard when you move me."

I told the woman that we extricate injured people from automobiles regularly and we would do so with care. I was so impressed by this woman's demeanor. She was so matter of fact. Not a hint of panic or fear in her voice or her actions. She knew she had sustained a potential life-altering injury and was strictly business.

Trooper Don Smith arrived a few minutes later and he proceeded to perform the scene details I had not had time to take care of. Suddenly I heard him yell, "Run!"

I looked up and saw a tractor pulling double trailers. The driver had lost control on the ice-covered highway. The entire combination was sliding sideways with the rear trailer in the dirt heading right for the damaged car. The only option was to leave the woman in the car and run! The woman's husband, the two children, and I raced for the desert. Miraculously, the trailer missed the wrecked car, regained control, and returned to the highway.

We used great care in removing her from her car, but this woman's worst nightmare had come true. She had severed her spinal cord during the rollover and would be paralyzed below the neck for the rest of her life. If anything similar ever happens to me, I hope I display as much strength and composure as that woman did that day.

Don't Stop Here

It was a typical hot summer afternoon in the high desert of Nevada. I was advised by NHP Dispatch of a Humboldt County deputy in pursuit of a suspected shooter. The deputy was chasing the man south on US 95, toward the town of Winnemucca. The Winnemucca police were establishing a roadblock at the north city limits to stop the suspected murderer.

The information I was given was that a Hispanic man, a farmer in the small town of Orovada, had just shot his boss and was fleeing in a grey Chevy pickup truck.

My sergeant was notified at home, and he asked that I check the city police roadblock on the highway to make sure it met legal requirements. You might think that setting up a roadblock is a simple task, but there are many laws governing temporary roadblocks, such as establishing a sufficiently large entrance and ensuring that cones, reflectors, and burning flares are all properly spaced.

After helping the police make a few changes to their hastily built, temporary roadblock, I proceeded two miles north on US 95. I parked my car at an intersecting dirt road, right off the southbound side of the highway. My plan was to pull onto the highway behind the pursuing deputy and stop all southbound traffic. If this armed man had already shot someone, the officers would need a mile or two of open roadway behind them if gunfire erupted.

I parked perpendicular to the highway, with the overhead lights on and the front of my patrol car facing west. I grabbed my twelve-gauge shotgun and took up a position behind the rear, driver's side fender. I monitored the progress of the pursuit on the radio until I could see the overhead lights approaching in the distance. The pursuit was high speed, and I was thoroughly expecting both the violator and the deputy to drive right on by me on their way to the roadblock, two miles closer to town.

But no! The shooter saw my patrol car as he approached my location, hit the brakes hard, and slid down the highway, leaving a long set of smoking, rubber-burning skid marks. While he was skidding to a stop, I kept saying, "No, don't stop here. The roadblock for you is two miles down the road!"

The pickup skidded past the rear of my patrol car and stopped ten feet beyond me, leaving nothing between me and the back of the truck except air. I had no cover whatsoever. With my shotgun aimed at the pickup's back window, I ran to the left rear corner of the truck and yelled for the man to put his hands up. He raised his left hand slightly, but from my position I couldn't see his right hand.

Not expecting the shooter to hit the brakes, Deputy Lamar Northrup, the pursuer, was barely able to stop before striking the rear of the pickup. I yelled again for the man to show his hands, and suddenly a three-year-old girl stood up on the seat, right next to the driver. I was quite surprised to see her, and she immediately rendered my choice of weapon worthless. The first three cartridges loaded in my twelve-gauge shotgun were double-aught buckshot containing 9 33 caliber pellets, each similar to the effects of a 9mm bullet at twenty-five yards. If I had to shoot this man, there was no way to miss the child. I tossed the shotgun onto the ground and drew my forty-caliber pistol.

Using the side of the pickup for cover, I moved right behind the front passenger window and peeked into the cab. Just below the shooter's partially raised hand, and resting on the seat at the little girl's feet, was a semi-automatic pistol. Without taking my eyes off the man, I opened the passenger door with my left hand, reached in, grabbed the girl's arm, pulled her out of the truck, and set her on the ground behind me.

By this time, Deputy Northrup, a large, full-blooded Paiute Indian who wore a perpetual smile, had moved up beside the driver's door. While covering the shooter, I told Lamar to open the door and pull the guy out. The man didn't resist this action and the arrest was made with no further problems.

It is not uncommon to get bad information when situations like this are happening. Sometimes they are reported by witnesses who are stressed out and don't really know the entire story. Other times, the information changes as rapidly as the event. It turned out this man shot at his rancher boss twice, and missed both times. So the charge was attempted murder. The little girl was the man's daughter.

Not long after this event, I was in court on the witness stand when the man's attorney asked, "Do you know if my client speaks English?"

"No, I don't," I replied.

"Well then, you don't even know if he understood you when you told him to put his hands up, do you?"

"No, I don't," I said. "But when a twelve-gauge shotgun is pointed at you, it doesn't really matter. It's kind of a universal language that means, 'Put your hands up!'"

The judge and the courtroom chuckled at my testimony, and it lightened the atmosphere. I was only assisting the officer, so I never found out what sentence the man received. But considering he missed, it probably wasn't too much time.

Ten-Five Oscar Meyer

Highway patrolmen seldom deal with sexual deviants. Occasionally we would arrest a rapist or molester wanted somewhere else, but sex crimes were not our forte. That is, until one day when I was advised of a flasher on I-80 near the town of Golconda.

A woman reported that a man driving a large, yellow, crew cab pickup had passed her vehicle at a high rate of speed. The man got a mile or so ahead of her, then pulled his truck over to the right roadway edge and stopped. In broad daylight, he stepped out of his vehicle with no pants on and fondled himself as she drove past. The woman refused to give her name but thought the highway patrol should be made aware.

I drove to Golconda but found no vehicle matching that description. This is a very rural region. Other than I-80, only one other paved highway is in the immediate area. However, there are many dirt roads. A local who knew the area would have little trouble disappearing. The next town east of Golconda is Battle Mountain, forty miles away.

Over the next few weeks, several more reports came in regarding the flasher. The victims were lone women and his actions grew progressively bolder. After flashing the women, he was now getting back into his truck and chasing after them. This latest action was frightening to his victims. None of the women wanted to identify themselves and none of them ever seemed to see his face. All of them provided similar vehicle descriptions. It seemed that the flasher drove a large, yellow crew cab truck that resembled those of the Nevada Department of Transportation.

Working day shift that month, I received the call when a sighting occurred. I would respond, and the flasher would already be gone. How did he hide a large, yellow truck in the desert so quickly?

We discussed the situation at our next district meeting. Lieutenant Tony Kendall and the troopers assigned to Battle Mountain attended. We thought the flasher might have a police scanner and could be keeping tabs on our locations, so we came up with a plan. From now on, dispatch would notify us of flashing incidents by using code words and the less conspicuous state mile markers rather than the large green federal ones. When a sighting was reported, dispatch would call Winnemucca and Battle Mountain troopers and tell them 10-5 (meet with) Oscar Meyer and give the mile marker of the sighting. We got a laugh out of that one and thought it might just work.

A few days later, the next report came in, and dispatch notified us using the 10-5 Oscar Meyer code. This time I was sure we would catch the culprit. Trooper Reynolds and I both raced toward the location in our fast, five-speed Ford Mustangs. Reynolds headed west from Battle Mountain while I sped east from Winnemucca, each moving in excess of 100 mph. We passed each other in less than fifteen minutes, and what did we find? Nothing! No flasher, no yellow truck, no victim, nothing. How in the hell did he disappear so fast?

A week or so later, another flashing occurred. This time the victim reported the flashing from her father's house in Golconda. I drove to the address and met with the woman. She had grown up in Golconda and was now living in Los Angeles. Finally, we had found a victim who could describe the flasher's face, height, weight and hair color. She was positive she could identify him if she saw him again. She was also able to identify the perpetrator's truck as a high railer.

A high railer is the term used for a railroad maintenance truck with train wheels added so it can travel on both the highway and railroad tracks. When I asked her if she was positive the man was driving a high railer, she said that her father had retired from the railroad and that she knew a high railer when she saw one!

So that explained how the culprit kept getting away. He was a railroad maintenance worker and knew every dirt road in the area. I doubt he would have jumped on the tracks to make a getaway, but he could have had he wanted to.

I met with my sergeant and relayed the information. We decided the next course of action should be to contact the local train master and ask for the names of track maintenance employees. The train master is the supervisor of Union Pacific Railroad operations in the Winnemucca section. When I met with him, he told me that he wouldn't provide any employee names unless he knew why we needed them. I informed him of the circumstances and advised him to keep the information confidential until we completed our investigation.

What a big mistake that was. A friend who worked for the Union Pacific called that evening and asked if I had caught the pervert. The train master couldn't help shooting off his big mouth. My suspect was a railroad signal maintainer. His physical characteristics and the vehicle description matched.

No longer in Nevada, my one and only witness had returned to Los Angeles. I got a photo of the suspected flasher and put together a photo line-up. A photo line-up consists of six photos, one of which is the suspect. The other five photos must be men of the same race, approximate age, and similar appearance to the suspect. I forwarded the photo line-up to the California Highway Patrol office in Los Angeles and an officer was sent to meet with my witness. The woman quickly and easily identified the flasher. The CHP officer sent me back the lineup and a report.

I interviewed the flasher at the Sheriff's Office and he denied it. In addition to my witness, I had several facts that added up to him being the perpetrator. The man worked as a signal maintainer and was the only railroad worker in a high railer pickup in the area. This was circumstantial evidence and not enough to convict him, but I also had my eyewitness.

I prepared a request for an arrest warrant for the flasher and again contacted the witness in Los Angeles to explain that her testimony would likely be required in court. That's when my case disintegrated. The woman, who had easily picked this man out of six photos, now said that she wouldn't feel comfortable identifying him in court. In other words, she wouldn't swear in court that it was absolutely, positively the man. I tried to get her to change her mind to no avail. No witness equals no case.

The I-80 flasher was never arrested, and within weeks the railroad transferred him out of Winnemucca. We never had a similar incident again. The flasher either carried on his behavior somewhere else or his forced move and his upset wife cured him of his strange sexual habits.

Recovered Before Dessert

In the summer of 1985, my first sergeant, Michael Curti, retired from the Nevada Highway Patrol. Mike always loved to cook and was excellent at it. Coming from an Italian family and loving Mexican food, Mike and his dear wife, Mary Lou, opened a restaurant. A few months later, Mike's Ristorante and Cantina opened in downtown Winnemucca. The food was good, Mike and Mary Lou were wonderful hosts, and the frozen margarita machine became our new best friend!

Winnemucca troopers and our spouses finally had a hang out where we felt comfortable, where we were not likely to see people we had arrested. We spent many a night at Mike's Ristorante and Cantina.

At the end of May 1987, I was working swing shift on I-80 just east of Golconda. Driving eastbound, I noticed two vehicles parked along the highway—a white Toyota pickup and a red Datsun 280 Z. Three men were moving items from the Datsun to the Toyota. I crossed over the median and notified dispatch of my location and the makes and colors of the vehicles. Afterwards, I walked up behind the three white males, one in his fifties and the other two in their twenties.

When I asked if they had mechanical problems, one of the younger men said, "Yes, we are traveling to Idaho and our car broke down. My uncle drove from Idaho to help."

While speaking with the men, I looked the scene over. The more I saw, the less I liked. I noticed that the Datsun's license plate had recently been removed, and the Toyota's California plate was hanging by one screw. A screwdriver and Nevada plate were on the ground next to the Toyota. I realized that I'd just happened to drive up in the middle of a license plate switch.

I backpedaled from the men to create distance and drew my .357 revolver. I advised the men to get their hands up where I could see them. The two young men followed my directions, but the older man just looked at me and said, "Oh, I'm scared."

"You should be," I said. "This is the wild west. It's one of me versus three of you. And if any of you make a wrong move, I'm shooting. And guess who will get it first?"

The older man slowly put his hands up. With my gun drawn, I directed each of the men to a position face down on the ground.

Back at my patrol car, I grabbed my microphone and advised dispatch of my situation. Asking dispatch for backup wasn't necessary. I knew they would have help on the way. I always read license plates to dispatch on any stops, but there were no plates to give. The Datsun had no plate on it, and the Toyota pickup was positioned in front of the Datsun where I couldn't see it.

As soon as I was able to convey the plates to NHP Dispatch, the bells went off. Without saying a word, dispatch confirmed a felony by signal. In felony situations, dispatch emits a high-pitched tone over the radio for several seconds. This tone advises the trooper of a dangerous, felony situation. It serves as notice to other troopers working to stop radio traffic until the trooper is safe.

I held the three prone men at gunpoint for a long time until backup arrived. The men were handcuffed, searched, and secured in patrol cars. I contacted NHP Dispatch and informed the dispatcher that we were Code 4 (safe) and that we had three in custody. When normal radio traffic resumed, dispatch advised that the California plate on the Toyota pickup belonged to a Datsun 280 Z, stolen in West Covina, California. The Nevada license plate belonged to George Shier, out of Winnemucca. It so happened that I knew Winnemucca

City Councilman George Shier. I asked dispatch to contact Mr. Shier and inquire whether his truck was missing.

A few minutes later, the dispatcher told me that she had located Mr. Shier at Mike's Ristorante and Cantina. George and Billie Shier had driven their Toyota pickup to the restaurant and that it wasn't where they'd parked it.

We learned later that the three men had been driving the stolen Datsun 280 Z when it broke down. One of the three hitched a ride into Winnemucca where they found Councilman Shier's pickup parked near Sergeant Curti's restaurant. They broke into it, tore out the ignition switch, hot-wired it, and drove the pickup back to the Datsun. They were switching their stuff and the plates from the stolen Datsun to the stolen Toyota when I rolled up fat, dumb and happy. I remember asking, "Are you guys having troubles? Do you need any help?" Duh!!!

I arrested the three men for possession of stolen property. Over many years of working the road, I caught dozens of people driving stolen cars out of California. California always wanted the cars back, but seldom the thieves. This was the only case I remember where California authorities prosecuted someone I had arrested for car theft. I got a trip to West Covina, in southern California, to testify against these thieves.

Mr. Shier thanked me for finding his stolen truck. He thought the Nevada Highway Patrol had provided great service by recovering the truck before he'd even realized it was missing or had time to finish his dessert.

My Best Friend's Brother

As a boy, my parents owned several acres of land on the Carson River west of Fallon, Nevada. We had horses, steers, rabbits, chickens and goats. My great grandmother, Esther Pawson Gibbs (we called her G.G.), lived in Fallon, and I spent a lot of time with her until she died. I was twelve years old at the time, and it broke my heart.

G.G. was born in 1886 and grew up on a ranch outside of Cheyenne, Wyoming. She was an accomplished horse woman and earned the distinction of being one of the first rodeo cowgirls of the west. A trick rider and relay racer, she won the coveted Women's Relay Race at the Cheyenne Frontier Days Rodeo in 1907. G. G. and my mother Charlotte (her granddaughter) were very close. Both loved horses, and between the two of them, I had no choice but to grow up a cowboy.

Horses were my major source of transportation when I was young. Most of my friends owned horses and we rode them everywhere. Fallon was a ranching and farming community, and a wonderful place to grow up.

After my sophomore year of school, my parents divorced, and I was moved from Fallon to Carson City. That was the end of my having horses. Carson High was much larger than Churchill County High. I moved from a small school, where I knew everyone, to a large school where I knew no one. I noticed something right away at Carson High School—cowboys were few and far between. Eventually, I found others of my sort. I met Michael Eugene Beck, a rodeo diehard, and the two of us became inseparable. If you found one of us, you found us both. Mike's family became my surrogate family.

Mike, his brother Bobby, and many of their friends were members of the Carson High School Rodeo team so I decided to join as well. Our group mostly rode bulls and bareback bucking horses. We traveled throughout Nevada to compete in rodeos and chase cowgirls. We had a lot of fun. Sometimes too much!

Fast forward thirteen years. I was in my eighth year as a state trooper, working and living in Winnemucca. My wife, Janelle, and I were raising three children. Mike worked as an executive for a large Reno casino and had three children with a girl from Yerington, Nevada. Bobby became a commercial mine exploration driller and had married his brother's high school girlfriend, Shannon. They had two children and lived in Winnemucca, not far from our house. Bobby and I renewed our friendship, and though we led busy lives, we enjoyed spending time together when we could.

Winnemucca and the rest of northern Nevada is the major gold producing area of the United States. As an exploration driller, Bobby drilled core samples for several gold mines located forty miles north of Winnemucca, off SR 789. The paved portion of this highway falls under the jurisdiction of the Nevada Highway Patrol. Beyond the pavement is the Humboldt County Sheriff's responsibility. Bobby worked for Long Year Drilling Company and took SR 789 to and from work every day. He drove a truck with large gas and diesel fuel tanks attached. The drill rigs operated miles from town, so hauling fuel was a necessity.

One morning, Bobby hit a range cow with his work truck on SR 789. That evening, Bobby stopped by my house and asked if I could complete a report of the accident. Bobby and I sat at my kitchen table, visiting, laughing, and enjoying each other's company as we filled out the report. Bobby had put in a full day drilling and was ready to get home when we finished.

Before Bobby left, he said, "I've had no alcohol for a year, my marriage is great, and I have two of the best children a guy could ask for. Life is really good!"

The next morning at 6:00 a.m., I began my shift at the sheriff's office. The dispatcher told me that there had just been a fatal accident on SR 789. Deputies were already working the scene, but I proceeded out to lend a hand.

I arrived at the scene, about five miles beyond the end of the pavement. The accident involved one truck occupied by two men. It had run off the left roadway edge, struck a large steel post, overturned, and caught fire. The truck came to rest upside down on its top and burned. Company markings and colors had all burned away. The deputy advised that one occupant had burned to death in the truck and the other had escaped out of the broken front windshield. The occupant who survived had left by ambulance to the hospital and was in critical condition with third degree burns.

I walked through the scene pointing out evidence of tire marks, rotation, and furrows in the dirt to one of the deputies. When the deputy told me that it was a drilling truck loaded with fuel, my heart sank. However, I reminded myself that several companies worked mine exploration in the area and this truck could belong to any one of them. I asked the deputy which company the truck belonged to, and when he told me, Long Year, I felt as if I had been punched in the gut. I asked if they had any identification on the two men. The deputy told me the man who had died went by the name of Sam. That was Bobby's nickname. Now numb with concern, I asked the deputy what his last name had been, and he said, "Beck."

With tears in my eyes, I returned to my patrol car and left immediately for Winnemucca. I knew Mike would be at work and I needed to contact him as soon as possible. I arrived at my office and called Mike's work number.

His secretary answered the phone and said that Mike was in a meeting. "He won't be available for a while," she said.

"I'm his best friend and I need to talk to him."

"Mr. Beck cannot be disturbed, but I will have him call you back when he's available."

"OK, let's try this. I am not only his best friend, I am a Nevada state trooper. His brother has had a very serious accident. I need you to get him on the phone now!"

That got her attention. Moments later, Mike came on the phone and said, "Hey, what's going on?"

"Bobby's been in a car accident."

"Not again! That dumb shit! Is he all right?"

"Mike, Bobby didn't make it through this one. He died this morning."

Mike was speechless at this point, so I continued. "You need to get to Carson City right away and tell your parents before they hear it from someone else. I am on my way to Bobby's house to tell Shannon."

After the call, I contacted the sheriff and made arrangements to go with him to make the notification of Bobby's death. I called my wife, Janelle, and told her the sheriff and I would be stopping on the way to pick her up. Shannon and Janelle were friends. With two small children at their home, Janelle would be needed.

The sheriff and I picked up Janelle and proceeded to Bobby and Shannon's house. I have already given too much sad commentary in this story, so I will skip the saddest part of all. Let's just say that out of many hard, sad days during my career as a trooper, this one was the worst.

There are serious lessons in our business that troopers learn quickly. One is that life is short and fragile, and it can end for any one of us at any instant. Poof!

Litterbugs

I never understood how people can litter. I have spent my life in the Nevada desert. It has been my family's home for four generations before me, and two after. Most aspects of enforcement were never personal to me, but catching people who threw cigarettes and trash out of the window was very satisfying.

More disgusting than trash and cigarettes are "Trucker bombs" which are one-gallon water jugs filled with urine. Often, they're left on the side of the highway for the whole world to see. Our highway workers are stuck cleaning up these nasty donations and they don't appreciate it. I caught many litter bugs over the years, and these are some of my favorites.

One evening, right before sundown, I was leaving the Humboldt County Courthouse in Winnemucca. This building housed many county offices, including the sheriff's office, justice court and jail. Across the street, opposite the courthouse, was a building owned by Judge Oren MacDonald and his wife Marge who had recently relocated from the small town of McDermitt to Winnemucca and owned a small dress shop in the front suite.

As I pulled out of the parking lot, I saw a black Jeep stop right in the middle of the intersection. The door opened, and a paper sack came out with a hand attached to it. The paper sack was placed on the street and the hand disappeared back inside the car. The door shut, and the car proceeded down the street.

These are the moments when troopers ask themselves, "Did I just see what I think I saw?" I stopped in the intersection and picked up the paper bag. Inside was a six-pack container with six empty beer bottles. Bingo!

I pulled the Jeep over and wasn't surprised to find the driver intoxicated. I taught DUI Traffic School for several years. A topic covered in class was how alcohol affected the mind and how the ability to make good decisions is one of the first functions to go. Getting rid of the evidence might have been a good decision, but not in the street right in front of the sheriff's office.

Judge MacDonald walked by as I was arresting the culprit. In Nevada, the judge sets the bail for misdemeanor violations in his township. I asked him what the bail was for depositing a six pack of empty beer bottles in the middle of the street. Judge MacDonald advised me the bail was one hundred dollars for the container and each individual bottle.

The man went to jail for driving under the influence of alcohol, having an open container of alcohol, and littering. With seven-hundred dollars added for littering, his bail was substantial.

You have probably never heard of a cigarette pig. It is my personal expression for a person who tosses cigarette butts out of the car window. Seldom do these pigs extinguish the butts before letting them fly. Cigarette pigs were much easier to catch at night. As the butt bounces off the pavement, it sends a trail of sparks down the highway. This is a clear signal to the trooper saying, "I am a cigarette pig. Please stop me and write me a great big ticket!"

In Nevada, it is against the law to throw any burning object from a motor vehicle. The cigarette pigs I caught over the years were always cited under the burning object law instead of littering as the bail was much higher.

I was heading home one evening on my dinner break. I was behind a blue, compact Toyota about a mile from my house. It was dark enough to require headlights which was probably the reason the driver didn't see my blue and silver patrol car directly behind him. The driver stuck his arm out of the driver's side window and dumped the entire contents of his ash tray onto the street. A cloud of ashes flew through the air and the unlit butts bounced all over the pavement. Oh boy! I couldn't turn my red and blue lights on fast enough.

When I walked up to the window, the lone older man said, "I'm sorry officer. I didn't know you were behind me!"

"Obviously," I said. "I'm sure you didn't!"

I was never the type to lecture someone before writing a citation. Most often, I would explain why the person was stopped, gathered the documents I needed, and write a citation. I did the same in this case.

I walked back to the car with a citation and explained the man's options to him, "Your bail amount for littering is $500, with a court administrative fee of $100, for a total of $600."

The man wasn't angry, but was almost in tears because of the bail amount. He said, "I don't have that kind of money. What if I pick up the mess?"

I told the man that I had no control over what the court would do. Any variation in the bail rested solely with the judge. I told him that I was heading home for supper and would be coming back this same way in about forty minutes. If the mess was cleaned up, I would note that on the court copy of the citation. As I cleared from the traffic stop, the man was picking up the butts.

After my meal break I returned to the location. The mess had been all cleaned up, so I documented that fact on the court's copy of the citation. I have no idea if cleaning up his mess made a difference with the judge, or if the bail amount was lowered. Most often I never knew, and quite frankly didn't care what the outcome of any citation or arrest was. I wrote citations daily and took people to jail when they needed to go. I decided early in my career that I would simply do my job and tell my story in court.

Please take the time to dispose of your trash properly. Many Highway Patrol troopers grew up in their home states and take littering very seriously. If caught, the chances of getting a warning are somewhere between slim and none.

Polygraph in My Pocket

Believe it or not, working patrol can be mentally tiring. All day, every day, troopers are looking at traffic, cars, license plates, equipment, radar controls, radar displays, drivers, passengers, pedestrians, light and siren controls . . . the list goes on. They are continually listening to a police radio, CB radio, scanners and music. Once in a while, troopers need to take a break and give their mind a rest. This story begins with me doing just that, driving on the interstate and not paying attention to anything or anyone for a few minutes.

I was on I-80 near Mill City, traveling east at the breakneck posted speed of 55 miles per hour. A grey, dilapidated van crept by my patrol car in the "fast" lane at 60 miles per hour. I glanced at the van as it passed. I had no intention of stopping the driver, but after passing, the van's speed increased a little more. Being a slow day, I reconsidered my position and decided to stop it. I intended to only warn the driver regarding passing a state trooper who is traveling at the posted speed limit.

Curtains in the back and side windows of the van obscured any view into the passenger compartment. I activated the overhead lights and noticed the van took an unusually long time before coming to a stop. I approached the van and saw that the driver was a woman in a bright red shirt while the passenger was a man in a white shirt. I hadn't been paying close attention when the van had passed me earlier, but I seemed to remember seeing the color red in the passenger window.

I instructed the man to give me his driver's license and he asked why since his wife was driving. The woman seconded his statement, saying she had been driving. I just wasn't positive which color I had seen when the van passed me. After checking that all their required documents were in order, I warned the driver to slow down and concluded the traffic stop.

I returned to my patrol car, contacted Elko Dispatch, and cleared from the traffic stop. The van accelerated, pulled back into the travel lane, and proceeded eastbound. I closed my eyes and asked myself, "What did you see when the van first passed?" The only color I could come up with was red. The woman in the red shirt must have been the passenger.

I caught up to the van in a couple miles and activated the overhead lights. I advised Elko Dispatch I would be stopping the van again. The van pulled to the right road edge, and I stopped behind it. I approached the female driver, wearing her bright red shirt, and asked her to please step out of the van and follow me back to my patrol car. Being stopped twice and being asked to step out of her vehicle kind of freaked her out. The man started to get out of the van. I asked him to stay in the vehicle, and he complied.

The woman, now visibly upset, followed me to the passenger door of my patrol car. I told her I stopped her again because I believed she had lied to me. She was pushing fifty years old with dark hair, and my guess was that life had been hard for her. I told her that I suspected that her husband had been driving earlier. Again, the woman claimed that she had been driving.

"Are you willing to take a polygraph exam?" I asked her.

"No one ever asked me that before!" she said.

"Well, I'm asking you now. I don't believe you are telling me the truth, and a lie detector will prove whether or not I'm right."

Anyone who has ever seen a polygraph machine knows that it wouldn't fit in a trooper's pocket. Nor would I have a functioning polygraph machine set up in a patrol car, although at times it would have come in handy.

After pondering the situation for a few moments, the woman finally burst out in an emotional voice, "Oh, all right! My husband was driving, and we switched seats as we pulled over."

"Was this your idea?" I asked.

"No, my husband has a suspended license for driving under the influence and he insisted we switch seats!"

As I walked to the passenger door of the van the husband rolled down the window, and I asked him to please step out. About three seconds after his feet hit the ground he was wearing steel bracelets and being searched.

Asked why he was being arrested, I told him, "Driving with a suspended license, obstructing and delaying a peace officer, and speeding 60 in a 55 mile per hour zone. If it were against the law to be a rotten husband, you'd be under arrest for that too."

I also could have cited the woman for obstructing and delaying, but I figured being married to this jerk was punishment enough. She didn't need any other problems in her life. I released the van to the wife who followed me and her rotten husband to the Humboldt County Jail where he became a temporary resident.

Get My Hands Up?

January 21, 1990, 6:45 p.m. I was the only trooper in my district working swing shift on a very cold, dark, winter evening. I had just gotten back into my patrol car after a dinner break at my residence with my wife and three children when dispatch advised of a property damage accident on I-80, twenty miles east of Winnemucca. I started that way.

On US 40, at the east Winnemucca city limits, I came up behind a gold two-door Buick. The Buick was traveling below the posted speed limit of thirty-five miles per hour and really attracted my attention when it crossed over the fog line (outer lane marking) twice. I followed the Buick toward the I-80 on-ramp to see if any more driving irregularities would occur. The Wyoming license plate check came back to a 1982 Buick registered to Willy's Quarter Horses out of Helena, Montana.

I followed the Buick for another mile and saw no more strange driving patterns and decided not to stop it. But as the Buick turned onto the eastbound interstate on-ramp, it caught my attention again. The Buick didn't accelerate in order to gain speed when entering the freeway; it actually slowed near the top of the ramp and stopped on the side of the highway. Now my curiosity got the better of me. I turned on my overhead lights, pulled my patrol car to a stop behind the Buick, and notified Elko Dispatch that I was 10-6 (on a traffic stop).

I grabbed my flashlight and approached the Buick. I saw only the driver in the vehicle as I walked up to the left-rear window. The driver rolled his widow down about halfway, and as he looked my way, he asked, "Why did you stop me?"

The driver was a large man, about sixty years old, wearing a heavy plaid coat, glasses, a fisherman's hat (pulled down low), with about three or four days growth of facial hair.

From my usual position behind the driver's door, I checked his hands and the interior of the car. I told him, "I'm Trooper Raabe, with the Nevada Highway Patrol. I saw you cross the fog line twice about a mile back, and you were traveling below the speed limit. Have you consumed any alcohol today?"

The man seemed very perturbed that I had stopped him and said in a cross tone, "No, I have not! I stopped at A&W, got something to eat, and am just traveling through to Montana. I noticed your car behind me and thought your headlights were real bright."

I didn't notice any odor of alcohol or any physical signs that he had been drinking, but he was very short and annoyed that I had stopped him.

I assured the man that my headlights were not on high beam and I asked to see his driver's license and vehicle registration. He told me that he had recently bought the car and handed me an odometer disclosure. Again, I asked him for his driver's license. He unbuckled his seatbelt and retrieved a small black wallet from his left, front pants pocket. He reached into the wallet and handed me a very old California driver's license which expired in 1966. The photo on the old license was a much younger picture of this same man, who the license identified as William Pittman.

"Why do you have such an old driver's license in your possession?" I asked.

"I keep it for identification," he replied.

"Do you have a current driver's license in any state?"

"Yes, I have a Montana driver's license, but I don't have it with me."

I asked Mr. Pittman for his social security number and he told me he didn't know it. I then told him to please remain in his vehicle and that I would be back in a few minutes.

I returned to my patrol car and contacted my dispatch center. "I need a 10-27 (driver's license check) and 10-29 (criminal wants and warrants) on William Pittman, date of birth 02-11-28, no social, with possible Montana driver's license."

I had a 100,000-candlepower aircraft landing spotlight in my patrol car, so the interior of Mr. Pittman's Buick was lit up like daytime. While waiting for dispatch to provide the information I requested, I could see Mr. Pittman shaking his head from side to side. Approximately fifteen seconds after my request, Elko Dispatch advised, "No driver's license match through California and Montana, no felony wants, and negative CJIS (criminal justice information system)."

Not feeling entirely comfortable with Mr. Pittman having no driver's license and not knowing his own social security number, I approached the Buick cautiously. As always, I stood behind the driver's door and window, forcing him to look backwards at me while we conversed.

"Sir," I said. "I stopped you initially because I thought you had been drinking. Now it seems we have a problem."

"What's that?" Pittman asked.

"You handed me a California driver's license that expired twenty-four years ago. Montana has no record of you having a driver's license," I replied.

"I have a Montana driver's license," he said.

"What is your social security number?" I asked again.

"I told you, I don't know it!"

Mr. Pittman's wallet was lying on the passenger seat, and I asked him to look through it for some other type of identification. Mr. Pittman was getting angrier in his actions, and I was getting more cautious (if that was possible at this point).

"I don't have any ID in my wallet," he stated.

"Pick up your wallet and open it," I said again. "There must be something in there with your name on it."

Mr. Pittman picked up his wallet, opened it quickly, and sat it back down on the passenger seat. "I told you there was nothing in there!" he said.

Speaking slowly and deliberately, I told Mr. Pittman again, "Pick up the wallet and open it."

Mr. Pittman, clearly annoyed and angry at my persistence, opened the wallet. I immediately saw what appeared to be the top portion of some credit cards.

"Right there," I said. "Pull out those credit cards and hand them to me."

Mr. Pittman pulled out the cards, and right on top of the pile was a Montana driver's license. "That's what we have been looking for," I said. "Hand it to me."

The photo matched this man, but the name on the license was William George Pearce. The hair rose up even further on the back of my neck, and I asked Mr. Pearce, "How many last names do you have?"

Mr. Pearce said, "I went through a bad divorce twenty-five years ago and I changed my name."

On guard, and watching Mr. Pearce's every move, I asked him if he had the vehicle registration. He reached into the glove box, with my eyes on point, and retrieved a Wyoming registration. I cautiously backed up to my patrol car and grabbed my radio microphone.

"Elko, #6144, I need 10-27, 10-29, William George Pearce, date of birth 02-11-28, social security number . . ."

Anytime a trooper comes upon a dangerous situation, like a stolen car or a wanted criminal, a tone is emitted over the radio. This tone alerts the trooper involved that he is in a potentially serious situation, and is a notice to all other troopers working through this dispatch center to stay off the radio. The involved trooper's number and location is given, so the troopers closest to the situation can respond to assist.

At 1941 hours, I heard a loud, shrill tone come over the radio and dispatch said, "#6144, Elko, 11-10 Frank, subject is armed and dangerous. Use extreme caution. I repeat, subject is armed and dangerous. Use extreme caution!"

In the ten years I had worked the road, I had been alerted by tones too many times to count, but it was never accompanied by "use extreme caution." When a tone was given, using extreme caution was automatic.

Mr. Pearce was a big man and was sitting in the driver's seat of his vehicle. His car was lit up like it was center stage, and I was behind him in the dark. If he tried to come out of his car shooting, initially he would have seen nothing but 100,000 candlepower of spotlight. I was in a much better position than he was. The driver's window had been partially rolled back up, with about a four-inch opening to speak to Mr. Pearce through. I drew my .357 revolver and moved to a position of darkness, away from my patrol car and the spotlight.

"Raise your hands up," I yelled at Mr. Pearce. "Get them up where I can see them."

There was no verbal response from Mr. Pearce. I could see his left hand, but his right hand was not visible to me.

"I can't see both hands," I yelled again. "Get them up where I can see them."

Mr. Pearce, still seated and facing forward, yelled back, "Get my hands up?" as if he was asking a question.

"Get your damn hands up where I can see them," I said.

Then a single gunshot sounded.

From my position, I saw Mr. Pearce's head slam backward and then fall forward. There was blood and spatter on the rear passenger window. I moved to a position behind my patrol car and grabbed my radio microphone, "Elko, #6144, shots fired, shots fired. I'm code-4 (ok) at this time!"

I immediately heard Trooper Wes Masterson advise Elko that he was twenty miles east of my location and 10-76 (in route). Every other deputy and city police officer working in the general vicinity of Winnemucca would already be on their way to assist.

Seconds later, I moved to a position behind the right front fender of my Mustang where I could see Mr. Pearce move slightly every once in a while. I advised Elko Dispatch, "It appears Mr. Pearce has shot himself in the head. Roll an ambulance and the coroner."

I stayed in my position and continued to observe Mr. Pearce until Humboldt County Deputies, Don Taulli and Leo Johnson, arrived at 1958 hours. Deputy Johnson moved into a position, with gun drawn, directly behind the Buick to provide cover. With Deputy Taulli on the left side of the Buick, and me on the right, we approached the passenger compartment. Mr. Pearce's head was tilted forward on his chest and he was no longer moving. From my position, outside and slightly behind the passenger window, I could see Mr. Pearce's right hand lying on the front passenger seat, still holding a firearm.

It appeared as if Mr. Pearce had expired, but we weren't willing to bet our lives on it. The doors were locked, and both Deputy Taulli and I were in a position to shoot if needed. Deputy Johnson asked for my nightstick, so with my left hand I removed it from the holder on my duty belt, and tossed it to him. He used it to break out the rear driver's side window, but was unable to reach the gun. I told him to reach in and pull Mr. Pearce's right shoulder back, to see if we could dislodge the gun from his grasp.

The plan worked, and the gun fell from Mr. Pearce's right hand onto the seat. I broke out the right front passenger window, reached in, and secured the firearm (a short-barreled revolver) and the situation stabilized.

As the cavalry arrived, the deputies and I took a few minutes to settle down and relax. Mr. Pearce was pronounced dead by the coroner at 2010 hours. At 2033, Highway Patrol Sergeant Doug Darlington arrived and turned the scene and the investigation over to the Humboldt County Sheriff's Office.

I was lucky that Mr. Pearce decided to kill himself rather than try and shoot it out with me. I ran across a lot of men in my career who thought they were bad, but most with bluster and wind. I ran across a dozen or more (that I knew of) who truly were bad, and Mr. Pearce was one of those.

So, what was Mr. Pearce's story? Well, he was sixty-one years old when I happened upon him, and his criminal history was long and distinguished. Mr. Pearce had been on the run from federal authorities since October 24, 1989. He was among eighteen defendants indicted in the District of Nevada (Reno), with numerous offenses related to importation and distribution of marijuana and the related laundering of marijuana proceeds.

The indictment was the result of three years of investigation by the Organized Crime Drug Enforcement Task Force (OCDETF) into the "Mancuso drug ring." This task force was comprised of agents from U.S. Customs, the Drug Enforcement Administration, the Internal Revenue Service, the Nevada Division of Investigation, and local Reno police agencies. The Mancuso drug ring was led by Squaw Valley resident and contractor, Ciro Mancuso, and was one of the largest cartels in U.S. history.

Upon issuance of arrest warrants for the eighteen suspects, Mr. Pearce (a pilot, enforcer and drug smuggler) escaped by plane from Reno's Stead Airport during the early morning hours of October 25, 1989. A search of Pearce's residence in Carson City, Nevada revealed a substantial amount of evidentiary documents and numerous firearms. Agents closest to the investigation sensed that if there were to be a violent confrontation in the execution of the search and arrest warrants, it would most likely involve Mr. Pearce. He was expected to shoot it out with police, or kill himself, rather than be arrested and go to prison.

William ("Uncle Bill") George Pearce had been a rodeo cowboy, a pilot, and a gaming cheat. He had been in Nevada since the 1960s and made a career of importing drugs into the United States. He provided his piloting skills to various groups, flying small marijuana-laden aircraft from Mexico to small, dry lakebeds near Kingman, Arizona. He later upped his game and flew larger twin-engine aircraft, loaded with drugs, onto dry lakebeds east of Carson City, Nevada, and then directly into the Carson City airport.

Witnesses described Pearce as being involved in several violent confrontations with Mexican authorities, including a shootout in Mexico with federal police at a clandestine airstrip. Pearce was said to have shot several of the officers before successfully executing his escape.

Pearce expanded his drug operations to southeast Asia, including Hong Kong and Thailand. He managed marijuana smuggling, processing and distribution operations at a "stash house" in Vacaville, California for years. The "stash house" was owned by Pearce and held under the shelter of a Cayman Islands "shell corporation."

Pearce was described by his associates as a man who would walk into a restaurant with thousands of dollars in his pocket and walk out on a meal check for the fun of it. He once threw acid in a woman's face for no apparent reason and attacked a man who owed him money with a hatchet.

As bad as Mr. Pearce was, I went home that night thanking him for killing himself and not trying to kill me. Training and experience carried the day for me, and I was very happy with the outcome.

An interesting side note: Ciro Mancuso, the head of one of the largest drug cartels in United States history, served only ten years in prison, and is the father of United States Olympic Ski Champion, Julia Mancuso. I guess he still had enough money left to pay for skiing lessons.

Alto! Alto Casaba!

While on patrol one evening, I saw a beat-up, tan Chevy cross over the center line into the opposing lane. During my highway patrol academy training, I learned that certain traffic violations are more common than others for drivers operating under the influence of alcohol and drugs. Crossing over the center line was near the top of the list—somewhere between sleeping through a green light and pulling over to urinate on the side of the road.

I followed the vehicle for a couple of miles and noted several other traffic violations. I activated the emergency lights, pulled the vehicle over, and contacted the Mexican driver. Dressed in work clothes and boots, he had the appearance of a man who worked hard. Unfortunately, he didn't speak English, and I spoke the same amount of Spanish. While trying to communicate with him, I noticed several indicators of intoxication.

Alcohol has the same basic effects on all human beings. It causes a flushed complexion, bloodshot and watery eyes, slurred speech, and uncoordinated movements. The next step in the process was to remove the driver from his vehicle and determine his level of intoxication.

Our department had adopted the National Standardized Field Sobriety Testing program. The new testing process began with a horizontal gaze nystagmus (HGN) test. HGN is the best alcohol test I have ever seen. When administered correctly, HGN is very accurate in determining if a person is under the influence of alcohol and can even be used to estimate the violator's blood alcohol level. However, this aspect of its use is not admissible in court.

To understand how the HGN works, you must first appreciate that when a person is intoxicated their brain is not functioning properly. Their brain tells their eyes, "I need you to look straight ahead so we don't run into something while I am in this condition." The eyes cooperate and say, "Ok, we will focus straight ahead until directed otherwise." The three-part test begins!

First, the officer holds an object at eye level in front of the person. A pen is frequently used for these tests. The person is asked to follow the pen with their eyes, keeping their head still. It is hard for an intoxicated person to do this seemingly easy task without several reminders. Most get the idea after a time or two. Or three. The officer looks at the person's ability to follow the pen with their eyes as it is moved from side to side. When a person is sober, their eyeballs will easily and accurately follow the pen. When a person is intoxicated, their eyeballs lag behind the object and are forced to play catch up. The result is a distinct jerk as the eyeballs move across the plane. This is called a lack of smooth pursuit and is strike one!

The second part comprises having the person follow the pen until their eyeballs are as far to the right or left as possible. Remember, the brain is trying to keep the eyes of the intoxicated person looking straight ahead. If under the influence, the eyeball twitches with a distinct, repetitive bounce. This is called nystagmus at maximum deviation. Strike two!

The third part is to determine at what position this bounce begins. With the tip of the nose being 0 degrees and the ear being 90 degrees, the eyeballs follow the pen from side to side. The nearer to the nose the eyeball bounces, the more intoxicated the person is. Onset of nystagmus before 45 degrees is definitely arrest time. Strike three and you're out. Or should we say, you're in . . . jail, that is!

Not able to converse with this Mexican man, I contacted my sergeant by radio and asked for his help. I advised him of my predicament and asked if he knew enough Spanish to administer a field sobriety test. Sergeant Jewett told me he spoke a little Spanish and was on his way to help. The man and I stood around staring at each other until my sergeant arrived.

When Sergeant Jewett arrived, he assured me he could help. The first test administered was the HGN. Sergeant Jewett stood in front of the Mexican man while I positioned myself behind Sergeant Jewett, looking over his right shoulder. This was my arrest. If the man was under the influence, it was imperative that I see the movement of his eyes. Sergeant Jewett pulled a pen from his pocket, put it in front of the man's nose, and said in English, "Watch the pen."

With my mouth right next to his ear, I said, "Sarge, watch the pen? Are you kidding me? I could have done that myself!"

Again, Sergeant Jewett said, "Watch the pen" as he moved it from side to side. Not understanding what to do, the man turned his head to follow the pen. Sergeant Jewett said, "Alto, alto casaba!"

Sergeant Jewett moved the pen to the side and once again the man moved his head instead of his eyes. Sergeant Jewett again said, "Alto, alto casaba!"

Shaking my head and rolling my eyes in disbelief, I spoke into Sergeant Jewett's ear again. "Sarge, I don't know much Spanish, but isn't casaba the name of a melon?"

Sergeant Jewett turned with a confused look and said, "By God, I think you're right!"

Laughter followed. The more we laughed, the more confused this poor, drunk, smiling Mexican man became. Maintaining any sense of composure was impossible. We laughed as we handcuffed the man. We continued to laugh as we searched him and placed him in the patrol car. I still remember this night many years later and I laugh. Alto, alto casaba!

Two Little Scratches

State troopers across the country investigate traffic accidents daily. Everyone knows of charges filed against drivers at fault for a crash. But many other reasons exist to determine the cause and document data from traffic accidents. The results may identify problems with highway design and conditions. For example, interstate highways now have rumble strips alerting drivers when their car leaves its lane of travel. Cause and severity of injuries associated with collisions have led to safer motor vehicle designs such as padded dashboards, collapsing steering wheels and air bags. Multiple collisions at one location can show the need for a change in traffic control or more enforcement.

Note: Many in accident investigation have changed the term traffic accident to traffic crash. Sometimes people drive into another vehicle, object, or person intentionally.

Nevada state troopers are proficient in accident investigation. They receive considerably more training in the field than other law enforcement officers. Even with advanced training, it became clear in the mid-1980s that accidents resulting in death, serious injury, felony charges and jury trials required more in-depth investigation than the average trooper was capable of. Unprepared troopers testified in court against professors, engineers and doctors of physics working for the defense.

The answer was to send a small group of troopers to Northwestern University in Evanston, Illinois to study and become Traffic Accident Reconstruction (TAR) experts. There has been an ongoing battle between police and academia over accident reconstruction. Many with college degrees looked down on the simple cop who received limited training in their field of study. The great equalizer is experience. While these doctors and engineers studied theory in the classroom, we troopers were working crash after crash. With the specialized training, we were able to stand up against these experts in court.

In 1987, I was selected to receive this specialized training. Before the reconstruction classes at Northwestern University, my class underwent many weeks of training in Advanced Accident Investigation, Technical Accident Investigation, and Vehicle Dynamics. These classes prepared us to take the Northwestern University Traffic Institute Traffic Accident Reconstruction Entrance Exam. Those who passed the exam (and not everyone did) attended this prestigious school.

The training itself is a story. Without a doubt, this course was the most difficult training I experienced as a state trooper. The instructors stuck a fire hose of information into your mouth and turned the flow on full blast. If you didn't swallow fast enough, you didn't pass. Occasionally our instructors answered questions with, "If you don't understand that concept, you shouldn't be in this class." Dozens of algebraic formulas were studied to work out vehicle velocities (feet per second) at each instant of a crash event from beginning to end.

We learned how to measure and convert collapsed heavy metal vehicle parts into energy and then convert that energy into velocity. We studied conservation of momentum and learned to determine pre-impact vehicle velocities by using the weight of each vehicle and post-impact velocities. The same result was reached both algebraically and by drawing parallelograms. Real case studies of accidents were used in class.

After reaching a conclusion, each student had the displeasure of testifying and being cross-examined by our instructors in a fake courtroom setting. Accident reconstruction can sometimes come down to the best guess based on experience. I like to quote my Northwestern

Traffic Accident Reconstruction instructor, Thaddeus Aycock, who said, "In accident reconstruction, two plus two is not necessarily f@#*ing four."

I certified as a Traffic Accident Reconstruction (TAR) expert and became proficient at applying the principles learned at Northwestern University. As an active member of M.A.I.T. (Major Accident Investigation Team) I traveled throughout northern Nevada working fatal and prosecution accidents.

Early spring, 1989, I responded to a double fatal accident on I-80 near the town of Lovelock. Often, I would arrive a day or two after a crash to reconstruct the events. In this crash I was both first on the scene and the TAR expert assigned.

When I arrived, I observed the remnants of a travel trailer covering both westbound travel lanes. Recreational vehicles (RVs) involved in serious crashes have a habit of disintegrating. I once asked an RV service tech, "What brand of RV is built best?" He said, "It depends on if you want junk or good junk, because they are all junk!" This trailer had taken one heck of a hit and came apart in pieces.

Further up the westbound side of the interstate was a commercial vehicle (tractor-trailer combination) stopped in the left-hand travel lane. The commercial vehicle had extensive damage to the right front of the tractor. In the median, between the remnants of the trailer and the commercial vehicle, was a pickup truck. The pickup truck, lying on its right side and pointing in a northerly direction, had extensive damage to the underside. The bodies of a man and a woman were crumpled in the pickup. Both had died prior to my arrival.

One of the worst things any investigator can do at a scene is to draw conclusions too early. It is necessary to keep an open mind and let the evidence lead you to a conclusion. Facts were obvious in my first walk through the accident scene. Both vehicles involved had been traveling westbound at the time of impact. The pickup truck, towing the travel trailer, was overturning onto its right side in the left-hand travel lane when struck by the commercial vehicle. The severe blow to the undercarriage of the pickup pushed the passenger bench seat upward towards the roof. This action resulted in the death of both occupants. Subsequent autopsy reports showed one occupant expired on impact. The other died soon after of positional asphyxiation, being too scrunched up in the wreckage to draw a breath.

Traffic accidents or crashes are often the result of a series of events. A reconstruction expert could spend weeks trying to work out every aspect of an accident—from speed of vehicles and transfer of energy at impact to possible reaction times, etc. Identifying the cause is the key. What evidence will explain how it happened and who is at fault?

I walked the scene again, taking photographs of roadway marks, debris, the area of impact, and the path of both vehicles after impact to their final positions of rest. These items and areas were located, measured, and drawn onto a field sketch. Many law enforcement agencies are now using laser mapping stations. These stations electronically measure and label evidence at the accident scene. A Computer Aided Drawing (CAD) program takes the data and produces an exact, detailed map of the accident scene. When I worked on the Major Accident Investigation Team, diagrams were drawn by hand and could take days to finish.

Long after the accident occurred, a car pulled up and stopped. Two men got out, walked up, and identified themselves. One was an attorney, and the other a civilian accident reconstruction expert. Both represented the trucking company involved. They flew from Nebraska in a private jet, landed in Reno, rented a car, and drove to the scene within six hours of the accident occurring. This gives you an idea of the money involved when a trucking company and/or its employee are at fault. When I cleared from the scene, the two men were locating, photographing, and measuring the evidence I had spent the last six hours on.

The commercial truck driver claimed he was driving in the fast lane. The pickup was traveling in the outside, slow lane. As he passed on the inside, the travel trailer swerved into his lane of travel. The right front of his commercial vehicle struck the left rear of the trailer. Then his tractor hit the underside of the pickup which was in his lane. Since the other driver and his wife were both killed, no one could dispute his story.

After reviewing all the data from the scene and inspecting the involved vehicles, I concluded that the evidence did not support the driver's story and set to determine which travel lane each vehicle was in during first contact. There are many ways to find this important place on the highway. Fluid trails from ruptured radiators or reservoirs. Tire marks called collision scrubs where a tire is forced downward into the pavement at impact leaving a distinguishing mark. Gouges caused by heavy metal vehicle parts removing roadway material from the surface, and scratches in the pavement caused by metal parts sliding across the surface, or all the above.

Of the many marks and evidence at the accident scene, two 2-inch-wide gouges and scratches on the highway surface told me who caused this accident. These gouges in the pavement were only a few inches long before they became lighter and disappeared. Centered in each of these two gouges was a single scratch mark. These two little marks in the right travel lane proved the commercial truck driver was at fault.

The following was the likeliest sequence of events:

A husband and wife left the state of Idaho on their first trip after retirement pulling their new travel trailer. They were driving westbound on I-80 in the right-hand travel lane. The commercial vehicle was westbound on I-80 in the same lane behind the pickup and trailer, traveling faster and gaining rapidly. The commercial driver attempted to miss the rear of the travel trailer by steering the commercial vehicle to the left. Straddling the line between both lanes, the right front of the commercial vehicle struck the left rear of the travel trailer. This action forced the rear of the travel trailer down into the pavement. The rear underside of the travel trailer had two 2-inch steel straps designed to protect the sewage holding tank. In the center of each of these 2-inch steel straps was a single ¼-inch-wide steel rivet. These two little marks proved the travel trailer was centered in the right travel lane when struck from behind. The commercial vehicle driver was at fault for this accident.

Any vehicle towing another is an articulated vehicle. They are connected in the center and the action and movement of one influences the movement of the other. When the commercial vehicle struck and pushed the travel trailer forward, the action caused the pickup to rotate in a counterclockwise direction. The pickup overturned onto its right side, in the left travel lane, in front of the speeding commercial vehicle. The front of the commercial vehicle struck the underside of the pickup, pushing the seat up to the roof, resulting in the death of two people.

Two little marks in the pavement proved the truck driver at fault. The positive blood test results showed the truck driver was under the influence of methamphetamines when he killed two people. I submitted the reports and requested a warrant for the arrest of the truck driver for felony driving under the influence of drugs. The district attorney decided against charging the truck driver.

When I asked the district attorney why no charges were being filed, he replied that, "the truck driver is from Nebraska and the dead couple from Idaho. The wreck didn't involve locals and a jury trial is costly. The family will get a million dollars in a civil suit."

This reasoning is why I never took a district attorney's decision whether or not to prosecute personally. My first summer working as a state trooper, we had two felony DUI accidents in our district. Both accidents resulted in the death of a passenger. Each driver was placed under arrest for felony DUI. One, a popular Winnemucca man received a suspended sentence. The other, a California man passing through went to prison. That is when I stopped caring about what happened to someone after I arrested them. I did my job and told the truth in court. If the judge let them go or gave them the death penalty, it was none of my business!

Months later, I testified at a deposition about this accident. The attorneys for the trucking company tried their damndest to dispute my findings, but they couldn't. The trucking company paid the family of the deceased couple a large sum of money.

Kidnapped?

I was patrolling US 95 one morning when dispatch informed me of a possible kidnapping at the Button Point Rest Area. I was forty miles away and started toward I-80.

As I pulled into the rest area, several concerned people met me. Travelers and campers using the rest area had come upon this strange situation and called the patrol. A mid-size, four-door sedan was parked at an odd angle, in a marked parking space, with the engine still running. A woman's purse, eyeglasses and a pen were on the ground within a few feet of the driver's door, which had been left open. It was a strange scene. It could've been a kidnapping.

All potential crime scenes must be protected, and evidence preserved. The person who first found the car advised everyone else not to touch the car or any items on the ground. As ridiculous as most crime scene shows can be on television, at least people are learning enough to leave things as they found them. I took traffic cones and evidence tape from my trunk to set up a perimeter around the scene.

The Nevada license plates on the car came back to a woman from Jackpot, Nevada, a small town made up mostly of casinos on the Nevada–Idaho border. Within minutes, our dispatchers had recovered the name, address, physical description, and place of employment of our possible victim. According to our victim's employer, she left work the evening before with plans to leave town for a few days.

While determining my next move, a commercial truck driver pulled into the rest area and blew his air horn. He held his CB radio mic in his hand, and I quickly grabbed mine from my patrol car.

"Hey, trooper," the driver said. "There's a woman lying in a ditch on the other side of my truck."

I moved my patrol car across the large parking lot and pulled in next to the truck. The truck driver said he saw the commotion going on at the rest area while driving by. Luckily, he caught a glimpse of a woman lying in the ditch. If he weren't so high up in his tractor, he wouldn't have seen her.

The woman was semi-conscious, dirty, and covered with brush. Not able to stand or answer any questions, she appeared scared and confused. The abandoned car belonged to the woman my dispatch center had identified. The Winnemucca ambulance arrived and transported the woman to Humboldt General Hospital.

After securing the woman's belongings and having her car towed to Winnemucca, I drove to the hospital. The emergency room doctor believed the woman had suffered a seizure. Apparently, she left her car, stumbled across the parking lot into the desert, and passed out in the ditch. I felt sorry the woman had gotten so sick, but was relieved she was found alive and not a victim of foul play.

They Never Saw It Coming

It was a sunny, summer, Saturday morning. Gassed up and finished with my morning coffee, it was time to hit the highway for another day. At 7:08 a.m. the Elko NHP Dispatch Center advised me of a 10-50 Frank (fatal accident) on I-80 at mile 179 eastbound. I had just gotten on the interstate at the 176 interchange and arrived at the accident scene within minutes.

I pulled in behind a Nevada National Guard tractor and flatbed trailer loaded with military equipment. It was the last vehicle in a convoy which had stopped on the side of the highway.

Crammed under the rear of the semi-flatbed trailer was the front half of a small red sports car. The sports car had hit so hard and stopped so fast, it was bent into a ninety-degree angle with the rear bumper and tail lights pointed toward the sky. With years of experience investigating accidents, I had never seen a scene like this.

After positioning the patrol car to protect the scene, I went to the sports car to check for injuries. Crumpled inside the wreckage and barely visible were the remains of two young men. Both men had died instantly. Several National Guard soldiers, including the driver of the tractor, met me at the car.

The semi driver advised that he had not been in the vehicle when the accident occurred. The convoy had pulled over to wait for other trucks to join their group. Several of the men, including the driver, were standing near the front of his tractor, talking and drinking coffee. They heard the crash, saw the tractor move a little, looked back, and saw the back half of a sports car pointing up in the air. They ran to the rear of the trailer and looked inside the car. They thought both men were deceased and there was no way to get them out, so they called the highway patrol and waited for me to arrive.

I got the driver's license and vehicle registration from the semi driver. The paperwork from the sports car would wait. The witnesses completed written statements while I took photographs and measurements of the accident scene. Evidence was limited to the roadway where the vehicles collided. Tire marks usually show the path of a vehicle or the actions of a driver before impact. In this case there were none. I walked back looking for tire marks where the car might have left the paved roadway and onto the dirt shoulder. No marks were found.

The tow truck arrived, hooked up to the sports car, and pulled it out from beneath the rear of the flatbed trailer. The two men would have to be cut out of the wreckage. It was going to be a difficult, delicate, gruesome task and not attempted on the side of the highway. We covered the car with a tarp and moved it to the wrecking yard.

With the help of the local ambulance crew and the Jaws of Life extrication equipment, the bodies were removed from the wreckage. Sometimes requirements of the job did not pay enough. Both young men had passports identifying them as Iranian citizens. The coroner took charge of the bodies. I returned to my office and contacted the Iranian Embassy in San Francisco, notifying them of the deaths of two of their citizens.

The next step in my investigation was to definitively prove the cause of the accident. Sometimes this part is impossible, sometimes it's easy. As I mentioned previously, the sports car left no tire skid marks or scuff marks on the pavement before impact. A common cause of vehicle accidents in rural Nevada is drivers falling asleep, and I documented this as the probable cause. The accident occurred early in the morning and my guess is that the passenger was sleeping when the driver joined him in slumber. Rumble strips are now commonly placed to alert drivers when they've crossing out of the travel lane, but at that time they didn't exist yet. It's also possible that the crash was intentional, but this is always difficult to prove without a note.

The speed limit was 55 miles per hour. If we assume the driver was operating the sports car at the posted speed limit, the vehicle would have been traveling at 81 feet per second. From the time the car first contacted the rear of the trailer until it stopped took less than one-tenth of a second. These two young men never saw the accident coming and perished instantly.

Have Tire, Will Travel

While on routine patrol one afternoon, I observed a young, white man hitchhiking on the eastbound side of I-80 about twenty miles east of Winnemucca. The man appeared well-groomed, well-dressed, and in his mid-twenties. Wearing a backpack, the man had a small automobile tire and rim leaning against his leg as he stood with his thumb out. In addition to traffic citations and traffic accidents, we also worked motorist assists. From breakdowns to flat tires, medical emergencies to missing parties, we handled just about anything involving people and motor vehicles on the move.

Motorist assists were a very important aspect of the service we provided. The only problem is that rural Nevada towns are so far apart it sometimes took hours to get stranded motorists running and back on the road. We didn't have a ticket quota per say, but there was an average number of citations issued per hour of on-view patrol. In other words, you were expected to produce numbers similar to the other troopers working in your area. Anything that took you away from ticket writing affected your averages, and you didn't want it to get to the point where your sergeant was asking, "What the hell are you doing out there? Driving around, smiling at people and wasting gas?"

When I saw this young man with the spare tire in hand, I remember thinking that it would be an easy assist. I would pick him up, drive him to his car (which couldn't be far), and get back on patrol in a hurry.

"How far away is your car?" I asked the hitchhiker.

"What car?" he replied.

"The car that fits the tire you're carrying."

"I don't have a car."

"Then why do you have a tire?"

"This tire helps me get rides. I've hitchhiked back and forth across the United States with this tire several times."

Hitchhiking in Nevada is against the law. Unless the hitchhiker is wanted for a crime or causes problems on the side of the highway, the law is seldom enforced. I wished this clever young man a good day and smiled as I pulled away.

I hadn't gone far when I noticed a car stop and give both him and his tire a ride. Sometimes a person just has to think outside of the box to be successful.

I Am Not Shooting That Cow

The job of a rural state trooper can differ greatly from that of troopers working in the city. One of those differences is dealing with Nevada's open range law. Rural Nevada cattle have the right of way on most highways. Highway warning signs declare "Open Range," complete with an outline of a cow. Drivers, by law, must watch for and avoid hitting cattle crossing the road. Those who do not heed the warning become the proud owner of a damaged cow and a dented vehicle.

I have investigated many vehicle versus cow accidents. Occupants can be injured when a cow or bull is swept off its feet, comes over the hood, and lands in their lap. But the blameless bovine usually gets the worst of it. The job of dispatching the poor beast to cow heaven and removing it from the roadway usually falls to rural troopers. All of our patrol cars had big steel bumpers attached to the front, and ropes in the trunk perfect for dragging cows.

Rookie trooper, Dan Hammill, was assigned out of the academy to the small town of Battle Mountain. Being Dan's field training officer meant two hours of overtime for me each day. I drove to Battle Mountain, worked an eight-hour shift with Trooper Hammill, and then drove home to Winnemucca.

Each trooper in Nevada, regardless of their assignment, had a patrol vehicle assigned to them. Rural off-duty troopers were called out to work regularly. Once, I was tracked down at a high school basketball game by the local police and told to contact Elko Dispatch. Now I was on call to respond to Battle Mountain, pick up my trainee, and instruct him in the duties of being a rural trooper.

About 0108 hours, my phone rang. Elko NHP Dispatchers were always pleasant in the middle of the night. "Good morning Trooper Raabe! Trooper Hammill has a 10-50 Paul (property damage accident). It is a non-injury, car versus cow on State Route 305, 25 miles south of Battle Mountain. I will call Trooper Hammill and tell him you will be picking him up. Your 10-41 (on-duty time) is 0108 hours. What is your 10-77 (estimated time of arrival) to Trooper Hammill's residence?"

"My 10-77 is 0200 hours," I replied. In minutes I was dressed and out the door.

I picked up Trooper Hammill who seemed cheery for his first call out—a little too cheery for me at two a.m. if my memory serves me correctly. But for a new trooper the first call out is an exciting event, especially if it's only car versus cow. Though a bit sleep-deprived, I did my best not to diminish the new trooper's enthusiasm.

We arrived on scene at 0223 hours. We saw a damaged passenger car stopped off the east roadway edge with a middle-aged man standing next to it. The car had been traveling northbound when it struck an extremely hard to see black cow. The injured cow was in a seated position with its butt planted on the center line and its front legs extended out in front of it. The cow, peacefully looking around, was watching our every move.

I directed Trooper Hammill to get the driver and vehicle information. Trooper Hammill walked back to my patrol car after securing the documents. I told him that he would have to shoot the cow and remove it from the roadway. I didn't notice any strange looks from Trooper Hammill after issuing my simple order, nor did I expect one.

A few minutes later Trooper Hammill asked, "Can I talk to you for a minute?"

I leaned into the driver's side of the patrol car and Trooper Hammill leaned into the passenger side. "Is something wrong," I asked.

"Yes!" Trooper Hammill said emphatically. "I don't want to shoot the cow."

"Why not?" I asked.

"Because the cow hardly seems hurt," he said. "She's just sitting there with her front legs sticking out looking around at everybody!"

"Well Trooper Hammill, shooting the cow isn't an option. If you haven't noticed, the cow has no back legs. They are gone, broken, kaput! They do not make wheel chairs for cows. There are no nursing homes where cows without legs can happily spend the rest of their days. You will shoot this poor creature and it will be happening soon!"

As soon as our brief conversation ended, a pickup came down the highway, stopped, and a man stepped out. Much to Trooper Hammill's delight, it was the rancher who owned the cow. I instructed Trooper Hammill to ask the rancher if he wanted us (meaning Dan) to shoot the cow. Trooper Hammill approached the rancher and posed the question.

"No that's all right," the rancher replied. "I'll shoot her."

Trooper Hammill had a smile on his face a mile wide and I'm sure he slept better that night knowing he didn't have to kill an innocent cow. I'm also sure Trooper Hammill, who spent over twenty years as a rural trooper, shot more than his share of cows during his career. It came with the territory!

Dangerously Lazy Cops

Most of the troopers, deputies and police officers I worked with over the years were good at their jobs and cared for their communities. But when I ran across a lazy one, it irritated me to no end.

The border town of McDermitt was a strategic place to enforce the speed limit and scan vehicles as they entered our state from Oregon. I often parked beside the highway in a dirt parking lot about fifty yards south of the border. One hot summer afternoon, I saw a large motorhome cross the border into Nevada. It appeared the driver noticed me because he started flashing his headlights as he headed my direction. The motorhome stopped next to my patrol car. An older white couple and their grown daughter got out of the motorhome visibly upset.

They explained that they had been traveling southbound on US 95 in Oregon when a pickup truck suddenly struck a small car they had been towing behind their motorhome. The collision knocked the car off the tow hitch and into the desert, but the pickup driver didn't seem to notice. The family pursued the pickup driver who was swerving all over the road. They thought the man driving was probably drunk, sick or injured and they honked their horn and signaled for him to pull over.

When the man stopped, the family tried to talk to the driver, but the conversation immediately turned confrontational. The man appeared drunk and threatened to get a gun out of his truck and shoot them. As he started for his pickup, the family quickly returned to their motorhome and headed for McDermitt.

My authority ended at the border, so I contacted my dispatch center in Elko and asked them to relay this information to the proper authorities in Oregon. Dispatch advised that the Malheur County Sheriff's Office in Oregon gave no time for the response of their deputy. Oregon State Police had no units in the area and couldn't respond. A Humboldt County deputy would respond in thirty minutes.

This area along the Oregon-Nevada border is so remote that deputies from the two adjoining counties in different states are cross-deputized and could legally enforce the law in either county. I asked for permission to cross the state line into Oregon and pursue the pickup driver, but was advised to stand by for deputies to arrive.

Thirty minutes later, a Humboldt County sergeant arrived and met with the family. Afterwards, the sergeant headed north into Oregon to locate the suspect and I stayed with the family. Fifteen minutes later, dispatch advised that the suspect had been located eight miles north of the border. The sergeant requested I drive the family to his location to identify the man. I obtained permission from my commander in Elko to enter Oregon and transport the family to the scene.

When we arrived, the Humboldt County sergeant stood on the side of the highway with a white male. A tan pickup truck was parked on the side of the highway. The right front of the pickup showed new damage and a big blue paint transfer. Every one of the family members positively identified the man as the one who hit their car and threatened them earlier. The man claimed he hadn't hit anybody.

The man had clearly been drinking, and the sergeant wanted to administer a field sobriety test. Field sobriety testing had recently undergone national standardization. All tests given were the same and began with the HGN test. Officers were required to be certified to perform the test, and the sergeant, uncertified, asked me to give this portion of the test. I gave this test often and didn't mind helping.

The man showed common signs of intoxication with a strong odor of alcohol. The sergeant stood directly behind me, looking over my right shoulder as I gave the test. Without going into detail, the man proved he was far above the legal alcohol limit. The sergeant, with the authority necessary to arrest this individual, decided to wait for the Malheur County deputy to arrive. Since the offense occurred in the state of Oregon, this made sense to me.

I loaded the family back in my patrol car and returned them to McDermitt. They asked me what would happen next, and I explained that the man would be arrested for a DUI and possibly charged with hit and run and vehicular assault. I told them how to obtain a copy of the accident report and then drove the seventy-two miles back to Winnemucca where I called off duty in my driveway just after 5 p.m.

Around 7:45 p.m., my dispatch center in Elko called and advised of a vehicle off the roadway near the intersection of US 95 and State Route 140. This intersection is 50 miles south of McDermitt where had I had spent a good portion of my day. I was the only trooper working that day, so back to work I went.

As I drove north of Winnemucca on US 95, I noticed a semi tractor towing a pickup truck heading southbound. The pickup was the same one involved in the DUI hit and run earlier in my day. I thought it odd that a semi tractor would be towing the pickup rather than a tow truck. I drove a few more miles north and passed the motorhome from the earlier event sitting in a wide spot on the east side of the highway. Now my curiosity got the best of me. I pulled in behind the motorhome and asked the family what they were doing there.

Very upset, they told me the man hadn't been arrested. Instead, he'd been set free and allowed to drive his pickup. They were parked in McDermitt when the man drove past them as he entered Nevada. They waited for a while, to give the man time to get ahead of them, and then started south towards Winnemucca. Near the junction of SR 140 and US 95 they saw him again where he had run his pickup off the road.

I was dumbfounded. The man should've been in jail somewhere. He had driven under the influence, caused an accident, left the scene of the accident, and threatened to shoot an innocent family who had just lost their car. Not to mention the jerk had ruined my evening. I should have been home with my wife and children instead of chasing this idiot around northern Nevada. But no, two lazy deputies hadn't done their jobs. Embarrassed, I could say nothing to this family except that I was sorry. I encouraged them to contact the sheriff of each county and file complaints.

I advised dispatch and returned to Winnemucca to find the pickup and the driver. I searched for a couple of hours with no luck. Never in my years working the road had I seen two law enforcement officers more derelict in the performance of their duty. I have worked with lazy cops, but these two took the prize. It wasn't my place to ask why this man hadn't been arrested, but I'm sure that nothing they could have said would have satisfied me. From that point on, I avoided the McDermitt sergeant as much as possible and never trusted him again.

My Colonel Was a City Troop

In the Nevada Highway Patrol, a trooper's personnel (P) number was assigned when hired. The three-digit number identified us and everything we did. Our radio call number, the license plate on our assigned patrol car, every report completed, and every citation issued used this number. The number preceding the P number showed rank in the following order: troopers 6, sergeants 4, lieutenants 3, captains and majors 2 and the colonel #2001.

Over the course of my career, my P number changed twice. The numbers were realigned and those left open by attrition were eliminated. My first number was #376, followed by my favorite #144 (it was easy to say), and finally #067. As a lieutenant, my radio call number became #3067.

When working in rural Nevada, we would hear and use our coworker's numbers on a daily basis. These numbers became as familiar as first names. What we didn't hear often were P numbers beginning with threes and twos. When we heard our regional dispatch center talking to a low number, the brass was moving through our area. In other words, it was time to get lost.

For the vast majority of my career I had the pleasure of working under some great highway patrol colonels. A state police colonel is also called the chief. To us he was the colonel, the chief, the big kahuna, the man in charge. Even though most of the chiefs I worked for were good leaders, it didn't mean you wanted to make yourself known to them.

Late one summer morning, while out at coffee, dispatch called and advised, "There is a report of a single vehicle injury accident, Interstate

80, twenty-five miles west of Winnemucca. Your accident notification time is 1046 hours. Two young women have sustained serious injuries. Humboldt County Volunteer Ambulance has been notified and will be responding. Twenty zero one is on scene and standing by until your arrival."

Injury accidents are not an uncommon traffic event. Rural troopers respond to calls like this several times a week. What was uncommon today? The colonel, the chief, the guy you don't want to see, was at the scene of the accident waiting for me to arrive. My patrol car, a 5.0 liter, 225 horsepower, five-speed Ford Mustang was fast. I arrived in record time.

As I rolled to a stop at the accident scene, I saw the colonel's unmarked patrol car parked on the eastbound side of the interstate. A wrecked car sat upside down in the median with two young women lying on the ground near it.

The colonel met me at my patrol car and said, "Hello, Trooper Raabe. We have two injured young women. I believe one has internal injuries and the other has a compound fractured femur. I came upon the accident right after it happened. Where is the ambulance?"

"My Mustang is much faster than the ambulance," I told the colonel. "The ambulance is coming from Winnemucca. It will be here soon!"

Every trooper in our state had been trained and certified as an Emergency Medical Technician (EMT). I grabbed my self-built first aid kit which included necessary items the state wouldn't supply—things like a stethoscope, a blood pressure cuff, airways, clamps, cervical collars and heavy-duty pads for bleeding. As always, my first task was to check on the injured young women.

While assessing my patients and checking their vital signs, the colonel asked me, "Raabe, where is the ambulance?"

"I'm sure it will be here in a few minutes sir," I said.

"How far out is it?"

"I don't know, but it is on the way!"

"Can you ask how far out the ambulance is?"

"If they are within ten miles, I can contact them on a car to car direct radio channel."

The colonel asked me to check even though I was working an active accident scene and caring for two injured women, along with other tasks needing my immediate attention. I returned to my patrol car and called the ambulance on the car to car channel. There was no response.

I told the colonel that the ambulance was at least ten minutes away, and he asked, "Would Elko NHP Dispatch know what their 10-77 (estimated time of arrival) is?"

My colonel, who I liked and respected, was now becoming a pain in my ass! "Yes, Elko NHP has direct contact with Humboldt County Ambulance."

Dispatch contacted the ambulance and advised that it would be on scene in ten minutes. I relayed this information to the colonel, who then asked, "Do you guys take care of injured people by yourself often?"

"All the time," I replied to what I thought was a strange question.

I had worked in the sticks for ten years, and it had never been any different. Then I thought about the colonel and his impatience. The man had worked his way up from being a trooper just like me. He must have handled hundreds of serious injury accidents.

That's when I realized my chief was a city troop! He had worked his entire career in Las Vegas and Reno, where the ambulance or fire department almost always arrives before the responding trooper. I experienced this first hand when I transferred to Reno later in my career. It was so nice to have someone else on scene to give aid to injured people.

I must have made an impression on the colonel that day because he wrote a nice letter about my performance to my sergeant. It was just another day for me, although one thing did change. When I heard the P number #2001 on the radio, I didn't try so hard to get lost.

Those Winnemucca Dunes

When I first started my career as a state trooper the legal Blood Alcohol Content (BAC) was .10 percent. Now .08 percent is the minimum level where a person is considered legally intoxicated. Most often, drunk drivers are much more intoxicated than .08 percent as was the case one afternoon on US 95 north of Winnemucca.

While doing paperwork at the Winnemucca office, the NHP Dispatch Center in Elko advised of a possible DUI driver. They had received a call from a woman who said she was being chased by a drunk driver. This woman, with her two small children, had come upon a green car stopped on the centerline of US 95 fifteen miles south of McDermitt. The car was partly blocking both lanes, so the woman stopped her car, a blue Ford, and honked the horn. This action apparently annoyed the drunk driver who tried to drive into the woman's car but missed. As the woman drove off, the man chased after her. Both vehicles proceeded southbound on US 95 at a high rate of speed.

I left the office and proceeded north on US 95 with my lights flashing and siren blaring. As I approached the first curve of the climb up Paradise Hill, I spotted a blue Ford coming towards me fast. Following close behind was the green car proving the chase was still on.

I slowed my patrol car to turn around and the blue car zipped past me. The green car came into my lane and would have hit me head on had I not quickly steered into the embankment. Back on the road, I caught up to the vehicles as they were pulling into the Paradise Bar parking lot. I slid to a stop as the drunk driver got out of his vehicle and headed for the woman's car. I yelled for him to stop.

He complied, and I immediately handcuffed him, searched him, and placed him into my patrol car. Ordinarily, I would have the driver take a series of tests to determine their level of intoxication, but this was one of those times that no test was required. This angry, drunk man had chased a mother and her children for thirty-three miles at high speeds.

I got the woman's personal information and witness statement, and calmed her down before she left. I read my prisoner the Nevada Implied Consent Warning requiring him to submit to a legal alcohol test. The man understood none of it, but the law required me to inform him. With that done, we headed for the Humboldt County Jail. The man was calm and talkative on our drive to Winnemucca. He had forgotten about the woman he'd been chasing.

A few miles north of Winnemucca, large sand dunes line both sides of US 95. As we passed these dunes, my prisoner said with slurred speech, "You know, those look like the sand dunes north of Winnemucca!"

"They do?" I asked in jest.

"Yeah, but that's a long way from here!"

Unable to resist, I asked, "Where are you right now?"

He looked out the window and said, "Somewhere between Bakersfield and Fresno."

Both of those cities are in California and hundreds of miles away.

My prisoner took a breath test at the jail and his BAC was .21 percent. That is over two and a half times the legal limit. Thinking he was somewhere between Bakersfield and Fresno on the way to jail, I would bet he remembered little of his ride the next day. Perhaps he visited the dunes he knew so well when he got out of jail.

Dopes Hide the Dope

The state of Nevada took a harder stance against illegal drugs than many other states. California, our big neighbor to the west, didn't take marijuana possession seriously at all. During my career, people caught with any illegal drug, including marijuana, went to jail.

Illegal dope could be found in several ways. Watching a cloud of smoke roll out the driver's window was an easy one. Or the fancy roach clip, covered with burnt residue, dangling from the rear-view mirror. One of my personal favorites was the baggie of weed sitting right on top of the vehicle registration in the glove box. In order to go home safe each night, cops must watch people's hands. When anyone reaches into any compartment, for any reason, the cop's eyeballs are going in there with them. Quite often, when a little dope turns up, there's more somewhere in the car. Such was the case one day while working I-80 west of Winnemucca.

I pulled over a yellow Ford van with California license plates. The car was occupied by two young men who seemed to be traveling with all their worldly belongings. I arrived as the driver's window came down and a big cloud of smoke rolled out. In those days, this resulted in immediate arrest followed by a legal, warrantless search.

I asked the two young men if they had more marijuana in the car. They assured me they had smoked the last of it. The car was packed with items for living, camping and traveling. Seldom in rural Nevada were there other troopers to help, so an arrest and search could take quite a while.

I placed both subjects under arrest for possession of a controlled substance and the driver for driving under the influence. I handcuffed and searched them, and then placed them in the back seat of my patrol car. I advised them of their Miranda Rights and asked if they wanted to answer any questions or make any statements. This is the time to say nothing, but most people can't resist professing their innocence. Many think they are smarter than the dumb cop, forgetting that the dumb cop does this every day for a living.

These two young men claimed that they had no more dope in the car. The angel on the cop's shoulder so wants to believe their story, but the devil on the other shoulder knows better. Not looking forward to pulling everything out of that car, I came up with an easier plan. I had a pocket size tape recorder in the front seat of my patrol car. Setting it to record, I got out of my patrol car and shut the door. After poking around in the car, I returned to my patrol car, grabbed the recorder, and played it back. The two desperados were shocked to hear their conversation being repeated.

"Where did you hide the dope?" asked the driver.

"He'll never find it. It's in my pillow case rolled up inside my sleeping bag."

Many years have passed, and pot is now legal in Nevada. I have mixed feelings about this change in the laws. Those who promote its use would have you believe that it's less harmful than alcohol. I don't buy it. It is just as dangerous as alcohol when drivers are impaired. It definitely kills many people's motivation and does lead to many young people trying harder drugs.

From a law enforcement perspective, legalization is positive. Countless police hours and energy have been spent chasing pot and pot smokers around. Cops don't get to pick and choose which laws they enforce. Arresting, booking, towing, and writing reports take a great deal of time. In recent years, these cases have been pled down to a slap on the wrist or dropped altogether, resulting in a monumental waste of our officer's time and efforts.

Not Pressing Charges

It's interesting interacting with people who think they know all aspects of the law. Many have watched cop shows on television their entire lives, most of which are ridiculously unrealistic. Some are jailhouse lawyers sharing bad information with their fellow inmates. Where others get the inaccurate information they spew out, one can only guess. Officers have a lifetime of studying, learning and applying the laws, and they still go to the books to get it right.

One of the most disgraceful crimes is domestic violence. I have never understood how anyone can strike their life partner, the person they are to love more than anyone or anything. Police and deputies respond to domestic violence calls daily. For state troopers, these types of calls are not common. Now and then, one half of a couple would be walking along the highway while the other half screamed at them. Occasionally, one half of the couple would be alone on the side of the highway where their spouse left them. Witnessing the crime of domestic violence was very rare for a trooper, but witness it I did.

One case occurred on a cold, snowy morning. Piles of plowed snow covered business parking lots and the sides of streets. I was working the early morning shift in Winnemucca and all of northern Nevada was white. After finishing paperwork at the Highway Patrol Office, I decided to patrol US 95 until the first accident of the day. I considered it a miracle I wasn't working an accident already.

I stopped at one of the few stop lights and noticed a man and a woman facing each other in a gas station parking lot. They appeared to be arguing. Suddenly the man doubled up his fist and struck the woman in the face. She landed five feet from where she had been stand-ing and fell butt first into a pile of snow. Blood flowed from her nose.

At once I advised Elko NHP Dispatch of a 10-10 (fight in progress) and gave my location. Sending a Winnemucca Police Department unit for cover would be automatic. Our dispatchers were top notch and babysat us over the radio every day.

As I pulled into the parking lot, the woman was still in the snow pile, and the man stood above her screaming. Not focusing on anything other than the woman, he didn't see me coming. For years I had practiced speed-cuffing in my defensive tactics class, and on this occasion I was skillful and lucky enough to handcuff this violent man before he even realized that I was there. While thrilled with my cuffing techniques, my joy was short lived.

As is often the case, the man's anger turned from the victim to me. I could smell the alcohol on him and there was no doubt he was intoxicated. His first reaction was to fight, but it's awfully difficult with your hands cuffed behind your back, so he tried another tactic.

With a smile on his face, he said, "You can't do anything to me because my wife won't press charges."

The woman, still seated in the pile of snow, said, "That's right. I'm not pressing charges."

These two lovers had played this game before. Several years later, domestic violence laws would undergo serious changes, but at this time many wife beaters still skipped prosecution due to their spouses refusing to cooperate. I had the pleasure of informing the wife beater and his wife that "pressing of charges" wasn't necessary on their part. This crime had occurred in the presence of a law enforcement officer and that was all that was needed.

"You're under arrest," I told the wife beater.

Both man and wife were shocked that their "I'm not pressing charges" defense didn't work. It had always been successful in the past.

My cover unit showed, and I collected the man and woman's identification. I drove my prisoner the two blocks to the jail and booked him. The woman, covered in blood and getting a shiner, refused medical attention. The police officer dropped her at the front door of the jail. Like so many domestic violence victims before her, she sat in the lobby and worked at getting her man released.

I'm sure she acted happy to see him when he got out of jail, and maybe she was. As sad as it is, many women live in these situations daily. I don't understand it, but I guess it's not for me to understand.

Chet, That's Good!

"Vehicle #1 drifted off the roadway edge. Driver #1 awoke and overcorrected to regain the roadway. Vehicle #1 re-entered the roadway in a broadside motion and overturned."

These brief lines are included in nearly all accident reports where the driver fell asleep while operating a motor vehicle. In any accident investigation textbook, you can read the same description of a motor vehicle in a side skid:

"Tires sliding sideways on pavement or dirt deflate and fold under the rims. The rims dig in stopping the vehicles forward momentum below its center of gravity. Momentum above the center of gravity continues and the vehicle overturns. The faster the vehicle is going when this action occurs, the more violent the result. As energy dissipates, the action slows until the vehicle comes to rest."

This is where seat belts earn their reputation for saving lives. They are designed to keep you in your seat until this violent overturning action stops. Occupants not wearing seatbelts do not fare well in these accidents. With or without seatbelts, I've seen how much luck plays a role in the outcome. This story is about a young man with a serious case of bad luck.

In our department, vehicle accidents were referenced by severity. 10-50 was the radio code for a traffic accident followed by the reported designation. P (Paul) meant damage to property, I (Ida) injuries, F (Frank) fatality. One morning, Elko Dispatch notified me of a 10-50 Frank on US 95 about forty miles north of Winnemucca. A vehicle had overturned, resulting in fatal injuries to the lone occupant.

When I arrived, I saw an older Volkswagen Beetle lying on its left side. I looked into the passenger compartment and saw one occupant. A tall, slender, blonde young man was still in the vehicle, lying on the driver's side door. I squeezed into the Volkswagen enough to check the young man for any signs of life and none were detected. The top of his head had been crushed.

Evidence at the scene indicated the young man had fallen asleep before losing control. The legal accident description was similar to the one mentioned above, except the Volkswagen had almost stopped before it gently overturned onto its left side. Not a violent flip or roll, just a slow-motion flop onto its left side.

Without a seatbelt to hold him in his seat, his head came out of the open window just enough to end up between the top of the door and the ground. Other than the fatal injury to the top of his head, he didn't have a scratch on him. Had he been wearing a seatbelt, this would have been a minimal property damage accident. With no seatbelt and no luck, this young man lost his life.

I covered the body with a yellow emergency blanket and then requested dispatch send a tow truck for the Volkswagen and for the funeral home to take possession of the body. The funeral home arrived first. An older gentleman by the name of Chet Seals was driving the funeral wagon.

Chet, in his seventies, had been a reserve deputy for many years until forced to retire. Now he worked part time for the local funeral home. The funeral home had a habit of sending one lone, old, out-of-shape person to retrieve bodies. This meant that troopers and deputies often had to move and load the bodies into the wagon.

Knowing I was the main body-mover for the day, I told Chet, "Back the wagon up near the head end of the body. We'll place the body on the gurney and slide it right into the wagon."

Chet got into the funeral wagon, fired it up, pulled forward, and lined up with the body. He put the wagon in reverse and began to back up. Everything went according to plan until Chet, coming on strong, couldn't hear me when I loudly said, "That's good, Chet!" The wagon kept backing. To my horror, the body covered with the yellow blanket was disappearing under the wagon's bumper.

Not wanting to panic old Chet, I yelled louder. "Chet, that's good! Stop!"

Chet kept on coming! No longer concerned with Chet's aging heart, I reached up and slapped the side of the funeral wagon and screamed, "Chet! Stop!"

Brake lights came on and the wagon stopped. The only part of the deceased visible from under the wagon was his tennis shoes. This young man, though deceased, had sustained minimal physical damage. Now he had been run over by a funeral wagon. Expecting more damage to the body, I could clearly see my future. Sitting tall in front of my sergeant describing how this happened. Or worse, explaining to the young man's family how this damage occurred.

I slowly walked up to the driver's window, now rolled down, and said, "Chet, move the wagon forward. Slowly!"

Imagine my relief when the body reappeared and there was no new damage. I strongly encouraged Chet to get a hearing aid, or turn off the radio, or do whatever the hell it took to hear me the next time I hollered stop. Luck was not on this young man's side that day. I, on the other hand, had been blessed with an overabundance.

AIDS Convention

In the late 1980s, the National Governors Conference was held at South Lake Tahoe, Nevada. Governors and dignitaries from every state were in attendance. Many Nevada state troopers arrived to fulfill security and driving duties. The conference, held in January, would likely be plagued with snowy, icy roadways.

Troopers from southern Nevada, who seldom drove in such conditions, worked eight-hour shifts as event and hotel security. Northern troopers from the high desert areas drove on snow and ice on a regular basis so we were assigned to transport the governors and other VIPs to and from the airport and several other locations during the event. Issued brand new Ford 4x4s and portable police radios, we were told to get lost until called. When called, we had to immediately respond to transport VIPs. I drove many people that week I had never heard of. I did have occasion to meet two I had heard of, Governor Patrick Robb of Virginia, and his wife, Lynda Bird Johnson.

The afternoon before the event, troopers arrived and checked into the Horizon Hotel Casino. Many of us cashed our per diem checks at the front desk of the hotel. Our next step was to find our rooms, change out of our uniforms, and proceed to the nearest bar. The main casino had a very nice, semi-circular shaped bar, with room for thirty patrons. Twenty-eight of those seats had been taken by off-duty troopers, while the last two seats directly to my left were occupied by an older couple playing video poker.

Two troopers walked up behind me and I heard one of them, Jack McKowan, ask, "Are you here for the AIDS convention? I just found out a month ago that I had AIDS."

At the time, Acquired Immune Deficiency Syndrome was an unknown, frightening disease and in the news often. Upon hearing this statement, the couple seated next to me gathered their money and drinks and vacated their seats. They couldn't walk away fast enough.

The two troopers sat in the now empty seats and ordered beers. A lesson in how far a thirsty cop is willing to go for a cold beer and a seat at the bar!

Careful What You Wish For

The last seven years of my highway patrol career, I held the rank of lieutenant. One day, while working as the Reno/North Lake Tahoe District Commander, I was contacted by the Franktown Homeowners Association President. The leader of the association was requesting speed enforcement in their residential area. According to the president, people were continually exceeding the posted speed limit, and the residents were insisting that something be done.

State Route 877 (Franktown Road) was in my district. Franktown, established in 1855 by Judge Orson Hyde, was in the southwest corner of the Wassau (now Washoe) Valley. The community of Franktown, part of the Utah Territory, supplied timber to the Comstock mines. At one time, hundreds of people lived and worked there. When the Virginia and Truckee Railroad was completed and opened in 1869, these supplies could be brought in by rail. Franktown died out, and now the area is known for its wealthy residents and very expensive homes.

I supervised six squads in my district, each led by a sergeant. Two day-shift squads, two swing-shift squads, one graveyard squad, and one Special Enforcement Detail (SED). The SED was comprised of hand-picked, hard-working troopers we called "hot pencils." That term you can figure out for yourself.

The sergeant in charge of the SED team was Patty Kinard. Sgt Kinard was one of the finest, most able, highway patrol sergeants I had ever worked with. Under her direction the SED team worked special events and traffic enforcement in problem areas. The SED troopers always worked as a team and had the same days off. Competent and professional, I could always count on them to finish assignments. From moving dignitaries, to catching drunk drivers, to complaints of speeding on Franktown Road, Sgt. Kinard and her team took care of it.

The speeding traffic on Franktown Road was so far down our problem area list it wasn't on it, but because we had a special request from the homeowner president the problem would be addressed. I told Sgt. Kinard about my discussion with the president, and she smiled and assured me that enforcement on Franktown Road would begin as soon as possible.

Two weeks later, I arrived at my office and found a note on my desk. The note read, "Please contact the Franktown Road Homeowner's Association President as soon as possible." I made the call and asked the president if the speeding problem was improving.

"What have you done?" he asked.

"I sent you the enforcement you requested," I said.

"You have to get them out of here. They've written all of us tickets. Me, my neighbors, and my friends. We've all been pulled over!"

I explained to the president that when we have complaints, we take them seriously.

"We don't have any problems," the president exclaimed. "Get them the hell out of here!"

With a smile on my face, I assured the president that I would have Sgt. Kinard suspend operations on Franktown Road immediately. "If you notice other traffic problems in your area, please give us a call!" I added.

I met Sgt. Kinard for coffee, and we discussed the problem area that was no longer a problem. She informed me that the SED Team only worked one day on Franktown Road. We drank coffee and laughed about how her team solved the huge speeding problem in just one day. If all police agencies had a SED team led by a Sgt. Kinard, traffic problems would cease to exist.

My Turn for a Ticket

It was a late summer afternoon in south Carson City, Nevada and my wife and I were running late to a party at a lieutenant's house. I should rephrase that. I've always had the bad habit of trying to squeeze two days of activities into one. I was running late, not my wife.

As we were traveling through the middle of the Washoe Indian Colony, Janelle said, "You might slow down. Tribal Police have been working this area recently."

I checked the speedometer and saw that it read 42 miles per hour. Then I looked in the mirror and saw that red flashing lights were already closing in from behind. Busted!

A young tribal officer approached my vehicle using good officer safety techniques. He stood where he could get a good view of my hands before stepping forward. I had to turn to speak with him and his gun hand was free. So far everything went by the book. The young officer's name tag identified his first name as Rafael. The officer asked for my driver's license and registration and explained why he'd stopped me.

From the way he phrased his questions, I recognized he'd been trained in verbal Judo. Verbal Judo is a set of communication principles and tactics that allow the officer to gain compliance and cooperation in others. It is a great technique that limits excuses from violators (like me) and helps cut arguments on the side of the highway.

Officer Rafael returned to his patrol car, completed a speeding citation, and walked back to my window in good time. After explaining the citation to me, I politely said, "I have written thousands of citations and I know my options."

Officer Rafael seemed surprised. "You're a cop? Where do you work?"

"I'm a Nevada Highway Patrol sergeant, assigned to personnel at headquarters. I hire all troopers statewide!"

He cursed and said, "Why didn't you tell me earlier?"

"Well, I was speeding. And you didn't seem interested in talking about it."

"Do you really do all the hiring?"

"Yes. From recruitment to selection. I do it all!"

"I applied to become a state trooper," he admitted in a sorrowful voice.

"Well then, we will see each other again," I said.

Everyone at the party teased me and joked about the ticket. I took it well because I was speeding and had it coming. Everyone needs to be taken down a peg or two once in a while.

On Monday, I went to my latest file of applicants and found Rafael. He had successfully completed his cognitive exam and physical agility testing and was now just awaiting a background investigation. Poor Rafael never dreamed I would hire him, and he couldn't believe it when I called him and offered him a job as a Nevada State trooper.

After the academy, Rafael was stationed in a rural post in northern Nevada and given the chance to become a state trooper. Regrettably, he got into some trouble his first year and was released from probation. Everyone makes mistakes from time to time. Perhaps Rafael was given another opportunity to live his dream.

Do I Look Like a Realtor?

After thirteen years as a trooper in Winnemucca, I was promoted to sergeant and assigned to the Reno office. I moved my family to Carson City, and twice every day I drove the forty-minute commute in my patrol car.

During my career, the main highway between Reno and Carson City was US 395, a very busy, four-lane road with miles of private driveways lining both sides. Most commuters between Carson City and Reno found the 55-mph speed limit on this stretch to be agonizingly slow. Residents entering and exiting driveways and side roads tried not to get killed.

For the highway patrol, this section was a continual problem with many serious accidents. We could not schedule enough patrol coverage, so troopers commuting to and from Carson City were appreciated. Troopers considered this stretch of US 395 to be a "cherry patch," a place where unlimited speeding citations could be written when their sergeant was on their fanny to produce more activity.

One afternoon while driving north towards Reno, I noticed a green Ford SUV traveling southbound at a high rate of speed. I activated the radar which showed the vehicle's speed to be 78 mph. As the Ford passed me, the driver, a white middle-aged male, looked my way. When I looked at him, he immediately returned his gaze to the front. I didn't see brake lights as he passed. As a matter of fact, he didn't slow at all. It's one thing to get a good radar reading in heavy traffic. It's another to slow a patrol car, turn around, and speed up to catch the violator.

Simple physics dictates that for one object to catch and overtake another, it must travel faster. After traveling over two miles, I drove around a corner expecting to see the green vehicle ahead of me. It was nowhere to be seen. I noticed a small cloud of dust on the dirt road north of the highway. The green car, containing the man I wanted to meet, was driving uphill into a residential neighborhood. He must have turned off the highway in one heck of a hurry!

I turned off the highway and drove up the hill. The road ended in a cul-de-sac and the Ford had stopped in front of a house with a "For Sale" sign in the yard. The same middle-aged driver I had identified earlier was standing next to the car, and I pulled up behind him with my overhead emergency lights flashing blue and red.

I had business written on my face as I exited my car and approached the driver. He pointed at the sign and asked, "Is this house for sale?" Not, "Can I help you?" or "What do you want?" or "Why are you here?" Instead, he looked right at me and asked, "Is this house for sale?"

The only reply I could think of was, "Do I look like a realtor to you?"

I informed the driver that I had checked his vehicle at 78 mph in a 55-mph speed zone. I collected his paperwork and wrote him a speeding citation. Nevada is very different from many other states. Few highways and roads exist where a violator can get away from a determined trooper. Unfortunately, that doesn't stop some from trying!

The Art of Interviewing

As the Reno Urban Operations commander, I supervised six sergeants who supervised over sixty troopers. Our area of responsibility covered all of Truckee Meadows and North Lake Tahoe. Way too much time was spent at my desk or attending meetings. As often as I could, I hit the highway to play with the troops. I say play because working the road is the best job on the highway patrol.

One night, a swing-shift trooper pulled over a car with four occupants for a minor traffic violation on US 395 north of Reno. The driver had a warrant for his arrest. I was patrolling that evening, so I arrived as the cover unit to assist the trooper.

While the trooper dealt with the arrested driver, I stood next to one of the three passengers and asked the young man some questions.

"Do you have any weapons in the car?"

"No," he replied.

"Is there meth in the car?"

"No."

"Is there cocaine in the car?"

"No."

"Are there any pills in the car?"

"No."

"Is there any marijuana in the car?"

"Not that I know of."

I am no rocket scientist, but it didn't take a genius to recognize the car had marijuana in it.

"Where is the marijuana?" I continued.

The young man appeared very surprised. "Well, if there is marijuana in the car, it isn't mine."

I stepped over to the other two passengers and said, "Your friend told me the marijuana in the car belongs to one of you. Would you like to tell me where it is?

The men looked at me in disbelief. Then they gave Mr. "Not That I Know Of" a dirty look. One young man confessed to owning the pot and told me where it was.

I drove away kind of feeling sorry for Mr. "Not That I Know Of." I'm sure he hadn't even noticed the difference in the answers he gave. I hope his friends weren't too hard on him. He didn't try to snitch.

That Darn Nevada Wind

Gusting winds are common in the Nevada desert. Rarely is the wind a factor in the death of a motorist, but it does happen. Major winds can cause dust storms in the desert, limiting visibility and resulting in multi-vehicle collisions. US 395 south of Reno is often closed to campers, trailers and commercial motor vehicles in high winds because they have a tendency to blow over. But has "That Darn Nevada Wind" saved a life?

One late fall day, I was traveling to Las Vegas on NHP business in an unmarked patrol car. A few miles south of the town of Beatty, I heard the local trooper come on the radio and advise Las Vegas Dispatch that he was on duty. He was en route to cover a lone Nye County deputy who had just located a murder suspect. The deputy's location on US 95 was a few miles south of Beatty and I could see the deputy's emergency lights two miles ahead. I arrived on scene and advised Las Vegas that I'd be out with the deputy.

I observed the sheriff's patrol car off the west (right) roadway edge behind a school bus which had been converted into a homemade camper. The old, dirty, beat-up school bus had seen better days. The deputy was kneeling behind his patrol car with his gun drawn. Fifteen yards off the west roadway edge stood a middle-aged white male. The deputy was shouting at the man to get down on the ground while he stood there with his back to the deputy, apparently ignoring his commands.

I took cover behind the rear of the deputy's car and watched as the suspect struck and lit a match. The Nevada wind quickly blew it out. The man lit another match with the same result, and another, and another. The man then turned around and I saw that he had three sticks of dynamite bundled and tucked into the front of his pants. The man was trying to light a fuse and blow himself to pieces.

Still ignoring the deputy, the man struck match after match which continued to be blown out by the wind. Regardless of how hard he tried, he couldn't get a lit match to the dynamite fuse before the wind extinguished it. Frustrated, the suspect went to his knees. With his last match and his back to the wind, he hunched over, struck the match, moved it to the fuse and . . . it blew out.

Out of matches, out of time, out of options, the suspect gave up. Thanks to "That Darn Nevada Wind" the man lived to see another day!

Where, Oh Where Has the Vice President Gone?

In July 1997, President Bill Clinton and Vice President Al Gore were invited to Lake Tahoe by Nevada U.S. Senator Harry Reid to discuss research and funding to insure water quality in the lake. At the time of the event, I was the Reno Urban Area Commander for the Nevada Highway Patrol.

Three weeks before the visit, I was assigned to assist the United States Secret Service lead team in planning transportation and motorcade routes. At the conclusion of the two day summit, Vice-President Al Gore and his wife, Tipper, extended their visit by five days to stay with friends who lived at Glenbrook, Nevada on the northeastern shore of Lake Tahoe.

While visiting their friends, I and one other Nevada Highway Patrolman and two California Highway Patrolmen were assigned to support the Secret Service and move the Gores by low-profile motorcade. The motorcade consisted of two unmarked Highway Patrol vehicles, one from Nevada and one from California, and three unmarked Secret Service vehicles. If the motorcade was in Nevada, NHP was in the lead with CHP following. The opposite was true when the motorcade crossed the California border.

In the early morning hours of day three, the Gores planned to meet friends and go on a hike. We drove the Gores to Squaw Valley, California where they met their two friends at the bottom of the tram. The four friends, accompanied by three Secret Service agents and a doctor, boarded the tram and up the mountain they went. We had no idea where they were hiking to, or for how long. We sat waiting at the bottom of the tram for several hours. About one o'clock in the afternoon, the Secret Service supervisor asked me if I knew where Soda Springs, California was located. Apparently, that was where Vice President Gore and his party were hiking.

"The trek from Squaw Valley to Soda Springs is a difficult fifteen miles," I told the agent. "It's roughly a ten-hour hike along the Pacific Coast Trail and drops 1200 feet into and out of the Royal Gorge."

The motorcade left Squaw Valley for Soda Springs, California. A command post was set up at the U.S. Post Office and there we sat. It wasn't long before we realized there was something wrong. The Secret Service commanders were unable to establish radio contact with the Vice President's party and they were beside themselves with worry, almost frantic. No one knew where the Vice President's party was, or if he was alright. Unless they had much better radios than we had, it was impossible to contact anyone at the bottom of Royal Gorge.

The supervisor sat on a rock with the number two guy standing next to him. Clearly, they were stressed. They were not allowed to lose the Vice President of the United States. Another agent took a photo of the two supervisors and said he was going to post it on the office wall back in Washington D.C. along with a caption below that read, "What was he wearing when you last saw him?"

It was a typical July day at the top of the Sierra Nevadas. Major clouds were forming, and soon there were going to be thunder storms and lightning in these beautiful mountains. As the afternoon wore on, so did the Secret Service supervisor's apprehension.

Finally, around four o'clock in the afternoon, they received a phone call from their hiking counterparts. The party had come upon a group of cabins called *The Cedars,* located in a beautiful area at the bottom of Royal Gorge, on the north fork of the American River. The story (possibly false) is that in 1905, *The Cedars* were deeded to a group of twenty-four, wealthy, old-money California families by a "good old boy" high in politics. Since then, this beautiful area has been a private resort, right in the middle of the National Forest.

Soaking wet, miserable and tired, the group walked up to a cabin, advised the occupants they were with the Vice President of the United States and asked to use their phone. They were invited in for tea, warmed up, and given use of the phone. Perks of the job, I guess!

Upon receiving "the call," our motorcade left immediately for *The Cedars*. The road drops dramatically for about six miles from Soda Springs/Serene Lakes to the bottom of Royal Gorge. We arrived at the cabin, at which time the hikers exited and said their goodbyes. As the group walked to the motorcade, it was very apparent that Tipper Gore was upset. She was wet, tired, disheveled, and extremely angry with her husband. We returned the friends to their car at Squaw Valley and proceeded to Glenbrook to tuck the Gores in for the night.

It was a day to remember. Escorting, losing, and finding the Vice President of the United States all in a day's work.

I Think a Warning Will Do

Occasionally we took a ride-along with us for a shift. Most often it was someone who had a professional interest in our activities such as reporters, judges, prosecutors, and our dispatchers. Nevada troopers have always worked as single units. With so few of us to cover the seventh largest state, two-person units were a luxury we couldn't afford. When you spent every day alone in a patrol car, it was a treat to have someone to ride with and talk to.

My three children watched their entire lives as I put on my uniform, strapped on my gun belt, and left the driveway in a shiny blue patrol car. I was never allowed to participate in "Take your child to work day" for obvious reasons. Towards the end of my career, I submitted ride-along requests for each of my grown children. My chief approved each one as they crossed his desk. Perhaps he thought a lieutenant couldn't get into as much trouble as a trooper.

My oldest son, Tim, home on leave from the Air Force, spent a shift riding with me. After a few hours and several traffic stops, it became clear that he had the interest, the demeanor, and the attitude to do my job in the future. Not overly interested in law enforcement at the time, Tim later became a state trooper. An exceptional Nevada State trooper to be exact.

My daughter, Corrie, was eighteen years old when she rode along with me. Her sense of humor and quick wit made for a fun night. A couple of years later she contracted West Nile Virus from a mosquito. She fought the disease, which almost killed her, for most of a year. Left with permanent damage, it has been the absolute worst part of my life.

My middle child, Mike, home on his short summer break from the Air Force Academy, rode with me one evening. Mike has always been a caring, friendly person who finds the good in everyone. I talked to Mike at the beginning of the shift about officer discretion. I remember telling him, "One of the reasons for traffic enforcement is to gain voluntary compliance from the motoring public. Citations are issued. However, if an officer believes a warning is sufficient, we have that discretion." I told Mike that during the ride-along I would let him decide whether to issue a citation or a warning.

We left our home in Carson City and were heading south on US 395 when I saw an SUV speeding northbound. I estimated the vehicle speed at 88 mph and clocked it at 85 mph in a 55-mph zone. A quick spin on the highway with red and blue lights brought the vehicle to a stop on the shoulder. I told Mike to stay in the patrol car and that I'd be right back.

The driver was about forty years old with dark hair. He was from California and traveling with his wife and two teenage children. I told the driver I had checked his speed at 85 mph in a 55- mph zone and that I would be issuing a citation. The man told me they were on vacation and he hadn't been paying attention to his speed.

I returned to my patrol car, grabbed my ticket book, and took out my pen as my son said, "I thought you said I get to decide whether to give a citation or a warning?"

"That's true," I agreed. "I did. But this guy was driving thirty miles per hour over the posted speed limit. That's a ticket if I ever saw one!"

"Well, not so fast! Is the man nice?"

"Yes, he seems nice."

"Is his family with him?"

"Yes, his wife and two children."

"Is he on vacation?"

"Yes, he is."

"I bet if you gave him a warning, he'd slow down. Isn't that the goal of enforcement?"

Shaking my head, I told my son, "You are way too nice to be a trooper! A warning? Are you serious?"

"I think that will suffice," he said.

I approached the vehicle still shaking my head in disbelief and told the driver, "I was definitely going to cite you for speeding, but my partner thinks that you'll slow down if you receive a warning today."

The driver also suffering from disbelief said, "He does?"

"Yes," I said. "He is much nicer than me!"

The driver, his wife, and two children turned around and looked at Mike in the patrol car and waved. The driver said, "Tell your partner thanks, and that I'll slow down for sure!"

"I will be sure to tell him," I said, and returned to the patrol car where I told my son what the driver had said.

"Mission accomplished," Mike exclaimed.

Maybe my younger son is not quite trooper material. Mike graduated from the Air Force Academy and is now a lieutenant colonel. He has flown well over a hundred combat missions in Afghanistan in a reconnaissance plane and now flies the F15E Strike Eagle fighter plane. He's also one of the nicest guys you could ever meet. Actually, a little too nice when it comes to law enforcement.

Do I Know You?

On a sunny, beautiful, Saturday morning, I was patrolling Alternate US 95. Near the small town of Silver Springs, I noticed a red sports car coming down a long, steep grade at a high rate of speed. I pulled the trigger on my radar and obtained a reading of 86 mph in a 55-mph speed zone. As the two-door sports car passed me, I spun around and took off after it. Seeing me, the driver slowed down to fifty-five and continued on.

I activated the emergency lights and puller the car over. The driver, a thin man in his late thirties was behind the wheel. A cute little girl, about five years of age, was in the passenger seat beside him.

I explained why I had pulled him over and he said, "You got me! It was such a beautiful morning, my daughter and I decided to get out of Reno and go for a drive."

I issued the man a speeding citation, and he signed it without batting an eye. After our business was complete, we stood outside the passenger door of his car and visited. He was a very friendly man, and we had a nice conversation. After twenty minutes, it was time for me to get back to work, so we said our goodbyes, shook hands, and went our separate ways. I was never subpoenaed for court, so I am sure he just paid his fine and got on with life.

Fast forward two years. My wife (Miss Coke bottle glasses) decided to undergo Lasik surgery. We are whitewater rafters and we were getting ready for our first trip rafting the mighty Colorado River, through the Grand Canyon. If my bride were to lose her glasses in a rapid or a flip, she would be totally helpless and unable to take care of herself.

The thought of wearing contacts in a sandy, windy environment wasn't appealing to her either. The trip is two hundred and eighty miles top to bottom. It takes three weeks, and the area is so remote, if something went wrong, seeing well could be crucial to survival.

Janelle took the usual preparatory eye exams, and the big day finally arrived. I needed to accompany her to the clinic that day because she would not be able to drive after the operation. We walked into the room to meet with the eye doctor right before the procedure began and you guessed it. I recognized him immediately. My wife's eye doctor was the guy I wrote the citation to.

We said our hellos, and while he was describing the procedure, he kept giving me the, "Do I know you" look. When the doctor left the room, I told Janelle, "I've met your doctor before."

"You have?" she asked.

"Yes," I said. "I wrote him a big speeding ticket. Do you want me to start looking for a Seeing Eye dog now, or do you want me to wait until we see how it goes?"

My poor wife gave me "the look."

"He knows he's met me," I said. "But I don't think he's figured out from where."

Even if he did figure it out, I knew it wouldn't have altered the outcome. But I couldn't resist having a little fun at my wife's expense. After thirty years of marriage, she must be used to my humor by now—but maybe not. The surgery went well, and Janelle was able to see the beautiful Grand Canyon without corrections or worry. Whew!

How Did This Happen?

"What the hell are you doing, you idiot?" screamed the nineteen-year-old kid. "You put the cream in the non-fat milk cans!" Learning to milk cows in Kalispell, Montana at 3:00 a.m. is a tough job. But it was especially difficult for a forty-year-old man, suffering the wrath of his over-bearing, young supervisor. Matt Paszek, built like a Sherman tank and strong as an ox, is about the last guy any sane man would call an idiot. It is a wonder the young man didn't suffer any injuries for his severe lack of judgment.

Matt walked outside the barn, into sub-zero temperatures, and asked himself, "How did this happen? Is this a bad dream? Have I entered the 'Twilight Zone?'" You would likely think the same if four short months before you'd been a respected Nevada Highway Patrol lieutenant supervising four sergeants and twenty-six troopers over a district the size of several northeastern states combined.

Four years after becoming a trooper, I met Matt who had recently been hired as a Humboldt County deputy. After working several cases together, and becoming friends, I talked Matt into applying for the highway patrol. Matt was hired, and after completing his second police academy, he was stationed in the rough and tumble city of Las Vegas. Over a span of several years, Matt gained a great reputation and was an up-and-coming state trooper. Raised in northern Nevada, Matt decided to leave Las Vegas and transfer back home. He and his wife, Debbie, and their three children, moved to the small community of Fernley, located thirty miles east of Reno.

Matt's reputation for hard work, fairness, and friendliness moved with him to the north. He did everything the patrol asked of him, and he did it well. He became a certified Traffic Accident Reconstruction (TAR) expert traveling throughout northern Nevada, taking on the most difficult investigations resulting in fatalities and felony prosecutions. As a TAR, he was called upon to calculate vehicle velocities and angles of impact, convert energy to speed, determine placement of ejected occupants, etc. Matt often taught a two-week course in vehicle dynamics and technical accident investigation to academy recruits and veteran troopers. On one occasion he was loaned out to the California Highway Patrol to help on a case in Placerville. A man had murdered his wife and staged an auto accident to cover it up. Matt's findings were crucial to the case, and the man was consequently convicted of murder.

Matt was promoted to sergeant and worked for me when I was a lieutenant over the rural district. A very hard worker, Matt took on any challenge or project I gave him. He served as a radar instructor and was called to be the interim Commander of the State Police Academy. He served over one year as an investigator in the Office of Internal Affairs and knew exactly how the section should be run. Rather than continue listing Matt's accomplishments, I will simply say that he was well-respected as a leader by any command officer he ever worked for, including me. He was later promoted to lieutenant and took charge of the same large rural district I had managed before.

So you ask, how in the heck does the state of Nevada lose an officer like this? Well, I am going to tell you a sad story. Since the beginning of time, there have been great leaders and there have been poor leaders. These days, good leaders are difficult to find, while poor leaders, the ones who couldn't lead a trail of ants to a picnic, seem to be plentiful. When poor leaders and command officers gain authority over others, the result can have disastrous effects on individuals and their families.

One day, four veteran on-duty troopers stopped in the middle of their shift to eat. During their meal they were dispatched to a call and had to leave the restaurant and their meal. One trooper, a NHP Association Director who had been at odds with some commanders over several issues, left without paying for his meal, the cost of which was approximately four dollars.

Why did he leave without paying? Well, he may have thought someone else had picked up the tab, or maybe he planned on returning after he handled the call, or maybe in the excitement he just forgot. Whatever the reason, does anyone really believe that a ten-year trooper would ruin his career over a four-dollar meal? The restaurant wasn't concerned, but by golly, justice must be served.

How was Lieutenant Matt Paszek involved in this event, you ask? Well, he wasn't. His involvement started right after the trooper's unfortunate crime came to light. Lieutenant Paszek was called to a high-level meeting filled with big shots. What was this important meeting about? Was it about terrorists striking the United States? Was it about future improvements to our beloved organization? No, it turns out this high-level meeting was about a trooper, who left a restaurant without paying for a discounted meal, and his incompetent sergeant, who wasn't there, but whose lack of supervision allowed this heinous crime to take place.

Lieutenant Paszek remembers the orders of the day. "Work on this day and night gentlemen. Go back in time as far as you need to, use whatever manpower, resources and overtime hours you need to get this done." Here, dear citizens of Nevada, were your tax dollars at work.

Having experience in the Office of Internal Affairs, Lieutenant Paszek was ordered to help with the investigation. During the meeting, Lieutenant Paszek leaned over and told one of the commanders, "This is totally unnecessary. Give me a sergeant to help and I will have this done in a week!"

The commander slapped him on the knee and said, "Matt, you don't see the big picture, do you?" The statement was followed by a wink.

"This investigation is a witch hunt, and I want nothing to do with it," Matt replied.

Over the next few weeks Matt did the bare minimum on the big investigation. His lack of interest and his understating of what the "Big Picture" really meant left him with a sick feeling. Lieutenant Paszek's lack of interest did not go unnoticed. One afternoon he was warned by a superior that he had better start taking an active role in this investigation.

The investigation that followed was Nevada's version of Benghazi. Months of dispatch radio logs and bi-weekly time sheets were scoured over looking for errors or omissions. Numerous troopers and staff were notified in writing to appear for interviews. All interviews were recorded, reviewed, and transcribed. The trooper was taken off the road and reassigned to a non-law enforcement position for months while the crime was investigated.

Matt was warned once again by a lifelong acquaintance who held a command position. "I just want to give you a heads up as a friend," he said. "You are losing stock big time, so you had better step it up and jump on board."

Then things began to get interesting. Matt received a subpoena from the defense attorney representing the trooper and his sergeant. Matt had no idea why he had been subpoenaed, but prior to the hearing he received three phone calls from someone in the Nevada Attorney General's Office asking him why he had been subpoenaed and what he was going to say. Patrol command officers involved in the investigation asked as well. Matt's reply was always the same, "I don't know why I was subpoenaed, and how can I possibly know what I'm going to say when I don't know what questions I will be asked?" Each and every one of these contacts could be construed as intimidating a witness.

Matt finally contacted the defense attorney and asked him the million-dollar question, "Why did you subpoena me?" It turns out that years before, this same thing had happened to Matt when he was a trooper working in Las Vegas. He and some other troopers were having a meal at a Denny's restaurant on the strip when they received a call from dispatch and had to leave in a hurry. After handling the situation, Trooper Paszek received a call from dispatch advising him that he needed to return to Denny's to settle his bill. Embarrassed, Matt immediately went to the restaurant and settled up. It was a shining example of a trooper not throwing away a sixty-thousand-dollar-a-year career over a three-dollar burger.

"Have you ever seen such a huge response over such a tiny event?" Matt asked the defense attorney. "I have attended more than one high-level command meeting regarding this investigation."

The attorney shook his head no and asked, "What high-level command meetings?"

After Matt had explained the situation, the attorney said, "Do you understand the consequences if you testify? If you honor this subpoena, you will be through."

"Am I being subpoenaed?" Matt asked.

"Yes, you are," the attorney replied.

"Will I be under oath?"

"Yes, you will be," he replied again.

"Well, I guess I don't have a choice then, do I?"

The day of the hearing finally arrived. Before entering the hearing room, Matt was approached in the hallway by two higher-ranking officers. "What are you going to say when you're on the stand?" one of them asked.

"I will answer the questions," Matt replied.

"Lieutenant Paszek, let's put it this way," one of them said. "Be very careful what you say."

Lieutenant Paszek took the witness stand and answered the defense attorney's questions. He related the events from his personal situation in Las Vegas years before. With no investigation, it was easily settled by stopping by the restaurant to pay his bill. Matt testified that he had worked in Internal Affairs for over a year and had never seen anything like this investigation. When asked of the costs associated with this case, Matt estimated that tens of thousands of dollars had been spent over several months to investigate an act which was most likely an oversight in the first place.

Several days after the hearing, Matt was contacted and told to report immediately to the regional office sixty miles from his home. When he arrived, he was met by two higher-ranking officers. They accompanied him into an empty office and told him to have a seat at the table. While not word for word, this is the gist of what was said to Lieutenant Paszek.

"It is apparent that your leadership abilities and management skills are in question. Your testimony at the hearing indicates that you think the actions of the officers involved were no big deal. We have several questions we want answered in writing and in detail, such as why you think it is acceptable for officers to steal, why you let your subordinates run wild without supervision, and why don't you support your command officers and their decisions? You will sit here until you have written the answers to all these questions in detail. Do not leave this office. Do not talk to anyone or go anywhere without permission."

Never, before this incident, had the leadership qualities of Lieutenant Matt Paszek been questioned. Troopers under his command worked hard and respected him greatly. They went to work every day knowing he had their backs.

Had there been a big-enough blackboard in his office, Lieutenant Paszek might have been forced to write, "I will be a good boy and I will lie under oath when my bosses ask me to," one hundred times.

Both command officers sat there speechless and glared at Matt until he finally asked them, "Are you both going to stare at me while I write this, or can I work in private?" Matt also requested copies of department rules, policies and state laws so that he could address their questions. The reference material was delivered, and the command officers left.

There Matt sat, fuming mad, distraught and hungry, trying to come up with words in support of people who would destroy anyone, at any time, who dared to question them or stand in their way. Later, two of Matt's troopers found him and asked him about a problem they were having. He told them, "Gentlemen, it's my turn in the barrel. The further you stay away from me, the better off you will be!"

Over the next few hours, one commander strolled through several times asking Matt if he was done yet and telling him to hurry up. Obviously, this commander wasn't allowed to go home until Matt was finished. One time the commander came in, shut the door and said, "Matt, you know exactly what is going on here."

"No sir, I don't know what is going on here," Matt stated.

With a shrug of his shoulders the commander said, "You had better join the group, or else."

"Or else what?" Matt asked.

"You know, Matt, anything's possible," said the commander.

Matt told him, "If joining the group means being like you and the others involved, I want no part of it."

Matt worked on his memorandum from one-thirty in the afternoon until close to eleven at night. Finally, he contacted his superior and said, "I have been here for almost ten hours, I haven't had anything to eat, nor have I gone to the bathroom, and the memo isn't finished."

Matt was told he could finish the assignment at home and turn it in on Monday.

When the memo was delivered, Lieutenant Paszek was surprised to find out that he was no longer in command of the rural district. Each day he was to report to a highway patrol office sixty miles from his home for daily assignments.

Justifiably distraught, Matt was watching the career that he loved, excelled at, and had invested close to twenty years in, going down the drain. In the preceding months he had seen numerous well-trained highway patrol command officers go down this same road, including me, followed three weeks later by one of the best colonels the highway patrol had ever seen. He knew this was the beginning of the end.

Unable to sleep, Matt went to see his doctor who put him on stress leave. He stayed on leave trying to figure out what type of work he could do to feed his wife and now five children as Debbie had recently given birth to twin girls. Matt received a letter stating he would need to pass a psychological evaluation before returning to work. There was no way Matt would win against these people, so he resigned.

Out of work, out of money, and out of luck, my friend and coworker Lieutenant Matt Paszek lost his house, filed for bankruptcy, and moved with his family to his father's house in Kalispell, Montana. That, my friends, is how a great man, a great father, and a great highway patrol trooper, ends up working for a nineteen-year-old mouthy kid, milking cows. To this day, my friend struggles to recover from this injustice, while the evil doers go about life receiving full pensions. There is a dark side to public service.

Some people, who claim to be leaders, are pros at holding everyone responsible but themselves. Many can cover their bases like national league shortstops. For those of you in leadership positions, employees are your greatest asset. Treat all of them the way you would like to be treated, even those you don't particularly get along with. Always correct employees' actions without revenge or anger. Don't use fear and intimidation as motivation. It only poisons the environment and will make for a very small retirement party when you finally leave. Recognize accomplishments and reward accordingly. If you show your employees genuine care and concern, you will earn their respect, and they will make you look much better than you probably are.

Hey Dad, What Are You Doing?

My oldest son, Tim, graduated from high school in 1994 and served five years in the United States Air Force. After coming home in 2001, Tim pursued a career in law enforcement and attended the Western Nevada Law Enforcement Academy. This academy, designed for students with full-time jobs, held class every weekend and several nights a week. Upon graduation, Tim worked as an officer for the Winnemucca Police Department. I was proud to have my son follow in my footsteps.

Two years later, Trooper Tim Raabe was hired by the Nevada Highway Patrol and stationed in Winnemucca. Tim was four years old when I started my career as a trooper in Winnemucca. I worked there for thirteen years before being promoted to sergeant and transferring to Reno. Troopers with prior law enforcement experience had to go to additional academy training and finish a twelve-week Field Training Officer (FTO) program. After Tim completed his training program, he hit the highway on his own. Rural Nevada troopers work alone many miles from any backup. That is where this story begins.

One afternoon, I was driving on I-80 with my wife Janelle and our daughter Corrie. A mile ahead of us was a highway patrol car. Tim was working day shift in this area, so I told my family that it was probably Tim up ahead of us. As we got closer, we saw the Nevada Highway Patrol car stopped behind a vehicle on the westbound side of the highway. As we passed, we saw that it was my son, and that he was crouched behind his passenger door with his gun drawn. One bad guy was lying prone on the ground while the other was still in the car.

Many people think troopers seldom draw their weapons while at work. In reality, it's common. When a trooper learns that the vehicle they're stopping is stolen, or that the person involved is wanted for a felony, the guns come out!

So there we were, in our pickup truck headed to Winnemucca just as our son was making his first felony stop as a trooper. I passed the traffic stop, crossed the median, and stopped the truck about a hundred feet behind Tim's patrol car. I grabbed a gun and told Janelle and Corrie to back the truck down the highway and wait.

I walked along the side of the highway towards Tim's patrol car. Aware of everything moving, Tim saw me coming and said, "Hey dad, what are you doing?"

"I guess, I'm your backup!" I replied.

"I'm not sure how the patrol feels about civilians helping," he said.

"Well, I did this my entire adult life and I haven't forgotten how. Besides, I'm the only help you have right now!"

Tim called dispatch on the radio and advised them that he had a retired highway patrol lieutenant on scene assisting him.

"What do you want me to do?" I asked my son.

"Let me get this other guy out of the car, then you can cover them while I get them handcuffed."

I watched as my well-trained son removed the other suspect from the vehicle to a position face down on the ground. As directed, when Tim was ready to approach the subjects, I covered the two men at gunpoint. Tim handcuffed and searched both individuals with textbook precision.

A deputy sheriff soon arrived as backup.

With help on scene and the two guys handcuffed and on the ground, Tim said, "Thanks dad!"

"You're welcome son!" I said before walking back to the rest of the family sitting in the truck.

My wife asked how it went, and I told her Tim had done great. But I wasn't so sure that he'd been happy to see me. His first few months on the highway patrol were filled with, "Your dad this…" and "Your dad that…"

Geographically, Nevada is the seventh largest state in the union, but the Nevada Highway Patrol is small compared to most other state police agencies. During my career, I worked in different regions, taught classes at the academy, held a patrolmen's association director position, and worked in personnel. I knew darn near every highway patrolman in the state, and Tim caught extra grief because of it. Now who shows up on his first felony stop to help but his dad. While the situation had been in progress, dispatch and several troopers were saying, "Wouldn't it be cool if the retired lieutenant who stopped to help was his dad?"

Tim called me later and asked how I thought he did. I told him that he was a well-trained trooper and that my only recommendation was to re-analyze dangerous situations afterwards to consider what might be handled in an even better and safer way next time.

Time has passed, and Tim has become one of Nevada's finest troopers. He has moved on to the detective division where every day he chases druggies and criminals. Tim has an uncanny ability to land right in the middle of trouble. Many officers are never involved in shots fired situations during their entire careers. Tim has been in two and has come very close to losing his life. Both times the suspect perished at the scene, and Tim went home safely to his family. You might think I am a little biased thinking my son is a fine trooper, and you would be right!

My Last Accident Investigation

Many traffic accident reconstruction experts find jobs working for attorneys when they leave police work. With months of specialized training, and years of experience investigating traffic accidents, they are more than capable of competing with professional engineers in the field of accident reconstruction. I retired from the highway patrol in July of 2001. I had offers to work for local Reno attorneys when I retired, but my wife and I already owned a business that was going very well, so I concentrated all my efforts there. My days of investigating traffic accidents were over forever. I never dreamed I would have the opportunity to work one more wreck.

I happened to be at my son Mike's house in Goldsboro, North Carolina when the accident occurred. My beautiful granddaughter Megan and I were standing on the lawn, in the front yard of his house. Suddenly, a lime green sports car zoomed up the driveway, turned onto the lawn, and disappeared around the corner of the house. The car was traveling at a high rate of speed, but other than the roar of the motor no other sounds were associated with the high-speed turn. Tires don't squeal when sliding on dirt and grass except in the movies. The green sports car failed to reappear from the other side of the house.

The vehicle was being driven by a young, white male with short, dark-brown hair. He was not wearing a shirt, but it was the end of summer and still warm outside, so it didn't seem unusual. The driver seemed at ease behind the wheel, too much so if you ask me. He couldn't have had much driving experience at his age.

My guess that an accident had occurred was confirmed by an eye witness. A young girl, slender, with the face of an angel, appeared at the front corner of the house where I had expected to see the sports car reappear. The beautiful girl was my other granddaughter, Katie.

"There's been an accident," Katie said. "The car just ran into my swing set."

"Where's the driver?" I asked.

"After he ran into the swing set, he got out of the car. He tried to move the car, but it won't budge. I think it's stuck."

I walked around the back of the house and sure enough, there was the green sports car. The young man had returned to the driver's seat. Its right front tire was resting upon the edge of the swing set support which kept it from moving. The back wheels of the car had spun in the dirt as the driver tried his best to get the car untangled from the swing set and make his getaway.

I hadn't been in a police uniform for years, but from the way I carried myself, others had guessed I came from that profession. As the witness and I approached the accident scene, the driver stepped from the accident vehicle and looked directly at me.

"What happened?" I asked.

The young man gave me a shrug of his shoulders and simply said, "I don't know."

"Do you think you might have been going too fast?" I asked.

All I got was another shrug of the shoulders followed by another, "I don't know."

"Young man, do you know how many drivers I have heard utter those same exact words over the course of my career investigating accidents?" I asked.

"No," he said.

"Too many to count," I replied.

I took photos of the scene, interviewed the witnesses, removed the sports car from the swing set and repositioned it on the lawn.

The young driver, identified as Carson Michael Raabe, age five and a half years old, climbed back into the driver's seat. As the electric green sports car leapt forward, his head slammed backwards as it usually did when he mashed the accelerator to the floor. My grandson disappeared around the corner of the house at breakneck speed with a huge smile on his face and not a care in the world. I could tell it was going to be a long afternoon!

Acknowledgments

I count myself among the fortunate souls on this earth who happened to find the perfect career, a job where you occasionally pinch yourself and ask, "Am I actually getting paid for this?" There is no substitute for finding your passion and making a living from it.

With very few exceptions, I loved putting my uniform on every day, climbing into my patrol car, and working the remote highways of my home state of Nevada. This book, filled with true stories, is the culmination of my career as a Nevada State trooper.

Every person who succeeds in life does so with the help of others. These mentors share their time, their knowledge and their experience. I would like to thank and acknowledge those who have contributed to both my career and this book.

First and foremost, I want to thank Sergeant Michael "Mike" Curti for being the best supervisor, teacher and friend a young, impressionable state trooper could wish for.

Thanks to retired Lieutenant George McIntosh and Major Rick Bradley, two exceptional state troopers. I was fortunate to have both of them as field training officers. They shared their knowledge, kept me safe as a rookie, and prepared me to work in an environment where backup of any type was considered a luxury.

Throughout my career, I worked directly under numerous state patrol supervisors and commanders, including a one-year assignment as a special assistant to the Director of Public Safety. Of those I worked for, a select few stood head and shoulders above the rest when it came to self-confidence, fairness, integrity and leadership qualities.

These exceptional command officers were Captain William "Bill" Souza, Captain Marvin "Marv" Davenport, Captain William "Bill" Goddard, Colonel G. Paul Corbin, Colonel Michael "Mike" Hood, Lieutenant Anthony "Tony" Kendall, DPS Director James Weller, Colonel William "Bill" Yukish, and Lieutenant Michael "Mike" Long. Thanks to you all!

Many thanks to my wife of thirty-plus years, Janelle Snow Raabe. She encouraged me to write my stories and spent many long hours staring at the back of my head and trying to talk to me while I typed.

My informally adopted father, Leland Roberson, was the first one to read the rough draft of my book cover to cover. He read it in two days and told me that he couldn't put it down. It's hard to tell if someone close to you really loves your work or just loves you. Either way, it saddens me that my dear friend Leland passed away before I could finish it. He is greatly missed, but his words of encouragement will last me a lifetime.

I cannot miss the chance to acknowledge my grandchildren, as they were also my inspiration for recording these stories. So, Spencer Jameson, Bailey Raabe, Ryleigh Raabe, Riley Houghton, Katie Raabe, Kalli Raabe, Megan Raabe, Carson Raabe, Tyler Steven Burridge, and Carley Houghton, thanks for being the cutest, smartest, best grandchildren Grammy Nel and Papa Steve could possibly have. Your great-grandmother Charlotte had another saying, "Every old crow thinks hers are the blackest," which in this case just happens to be true.

This part-time project took several years of writing, rewriting, and rewriting again. After using a self-editing computer program, I was recommended an editor by the name of Jon Gosch. What great advice. Jon has been fantastic to work with and countless emails have passed between us. I was very rough around the edges and made Jon earn his pay. He suggested changes to script, punctuation and sentence structure in red highlight. Many of my first stories were returned to me looking as if they had died a terrible death. Jon's advice and suggestions have made me a better writer and helped make this book a success.

The final thanks go to Russel Davis and his team at Gray Dog Press in Spokane, Washington. One day I was attending a craft fair in Yuma and met with a man who had written and published a book. I had seen several self-published books at events like this, but none that matched the quality of his. The book was published by Gray Dog Press, and Russel soon became the first professional I contacted about my book. I jokingly explained to Russel that I had already been a professional writer for years—if traffic citations, arrest reports and warrant requests count. He never said they didn't count, but he knew I was a rookie when it came to writing a book. Russel's advice, direction and publishing skills have been instrumental.